WONDERS
OF THE
WORLD

WONDERS
OF THE
WORLD

ROLAND GÖÖCK

Translated from the German by
KATE REDDICK

HAMLYN
London · New York · Sydney · Toronto

Contents

Alle Wunder dieser Welt
© Copyright 1968 by
Verlagsgruppe Bertelsmann GmbH
Bertelsmann Sachbuchverlag
Gütersloh

Wonders of the World
Published by
The Hamlyn Publishing Group Ltd
London . New York . Sydney . Toronto
Hamlyn House
Feltham, Middlesex, England

English translation
© Copyright The Hamlyn Publishing Group
All rights reserved

ISBN 0 600 39253 8

Photoset by BAS Printers Limited, Wallop,
Hampshire
Reproduced and printed in Spain
by Printer, Industria Grafica S.A. Tuset 19
Barcelona, San Vicente Dels Horts 1972
Depósito Legal B 27651–1972
Mohn Gordon Ltd. London

Introduction
The wonders of this world   5

Wonders of Antiquity
The Colossi of the Pharaohs   8
The Hanging Gardens   12
The Temple of Artemis at Ephesus   14
The Mausoleum at Halicarnassus   15
The Colossus of Rhodes   16
The Pharos of Alexandria   17
The Statue of Zeus at Olympia   17

Wonders of Europe
Cologne Cathedral   20
Glockner-Kaprun   24
The Atom um   26
Holland's Delta Plan   28
The Escorial   32
The Alhambra   36
Venice   40
Milan Cathedral   44
Ancient Rome   48
St Peter's in Rome   52
Vesuvius   56
The Acropolis   60
The Mont Blanc Tunnel   64
The Eiffel Tower   68
Arc de Triomphe   72
Versailles   76
La Rance Tidal Power Station   80
Ronchamp   84
Stonehenge   88
Surtsey   90
Thingvellir   94
Postojna Caves   96
The Kremlin   98

Wonders of Asia
Hagia Sophia   104
Baalbek   108
The Omayyad Mosque   112
Jerusalem   116
The Dead Sea   122
The Taj Mahal   124
The Temples of Bangkok   128
The Shwe Dagon Pagoda   132
Angkor   136
Nikko   140
Dai Butsu of Kamakura   144
The Great Wall of China   148
Borobudur   154

Wonders of Africa
The Suez Canal   160
Abu Simbel   164
The Aswan High Dam   168
Victoria Falls   170
Kariba Dam   174
Big Hole   178

Wonders of America
The St Lawrence Seaway   182
Niagara Falls   184
Habitat   188
The Skyline of New York   192
Mammoth Caves   198
Mount Rushmore   200
The Grand Canyon   204
Mount Palomar   208
Yellowstone National Park   212
Cape Kennedy   216
The Golden Gate Bridge   222
Marina City   226
Chichen Itza   228
The Panama Canal   232
Rio de Janeiro   236
Brasilia   240
Iguaçu Falls   244
Machu Picchu   248

Index   252
Acknowledgments   255

THE WONDERS OF THIS WORLD

hat is a 'wonder of the world'? There is obviously no unequivocal definition of such a concept. All definitions lean on the famous list of the seven wonders of the ancient world which for over 2,000 years have been regarded as the most amazing, most sensational, most beautiful, most ⸱erable and most grandiose human achievements because of ⸱r size and splendour. The Greeks, compiled the first list, con-⸱ing the Pyramids of Gizeh, the Hanging Gardens of Babylon, ⸱ Temple of Artemis at Ephesus, the Pharos of Alexandria and the ⸱ue of Zeus at Olympia were not so pretentious as to talk of ⸱nders of the world'. They described those things which, in their ⸱ion, were the most significant achievements of their time as ⸱epta theamata, which means merely 'seven things worth seeing'. ⸱as only the admiration of the Middle Ages that turned them ⸱ 'wonders of the world'. Following the Greek example, people ⸱. in the past often suggested contemporary achievements to ⸱ace the dilapidated ruins of antiquity. For example, a list of the ⸱ders of the city of Rome was compiled in the year AD 448. It ⸱ded the sewers, the aqueducts, the hot springs and the Colos-⸱n and many other buildings. At about the same time a list ⸱ drawn up of the seven most important churches of Rome ⸱ch it was the duty of every pilgrim to Rome to make a point of ⸱ing.

⸱uring the age of travel, discovery and conquest the horizons of ⸱pe began to broaden. Sensational reports came back describing ⸱ golden palaces, mighty forts and gigantic temples of distant ⸱s, but it was not until the seventeenth century that the first ⸱d-wide list of the wonders was compiled. It included the ⸱elain tower of Nanking, the Great Wall of China, the Hagia ⸱hia in Istanbul, the Leaning Tower of Pisa, the catacombs of ⸱e, the Colosseum Rome and Stonehenge in England. However, ⸱le noticed that the world had considerably more than seven ⸱worthy sites to offer! Journalism and the development of new ⸱ems of transport played an important part in broadening the ⸱ook of Europeans: as it became easier to travel to distant lands, ⸱news of amazing sights to be seen spread faster. Thomas Cook, ⸱world's first travel agent, knew exactly what he was doing ⸱n he took his first group of tourists to see the greatest sights in ⸱world. He planned his tours in a methodical, businesslike way. ⸱example, because he found it was too strenuous for his charges ⸱ake the ascent of Vesuvius on foot he had a cable railway built ⸱ it developed into a very successful enterprise. Because there ⸱ no regular or suitable means of crossing the Nile to reach the temples of Abu Simbel, Cook organized a ferry.

Cook quite rightly recognized that not only architectural and technological but also natural wonders were of interest. During the stagecoach era, to say nothing of preceding centuries, the average traveller looked on nature as an enemy. Mountains were not beautiful, merely an obstacle to travel; waterfalls demonstrated at best the fury of nature; volcanoes, which could erupt at any moment, were to be avoided at all costs. Cook included the breath-taking creations of nature in his list of sights which nobody should miss seeing.

Newspapers, travel reports, photography and, later, films and television popularized the creations of man and nature. Sea and air travel brought the wonders of the world within reach. Did that make them any the less wonderful? No: on the contrary, man's interest in the world grows greater year by year. At the turn of the century Ernst von Hesse-Wartegg, having devoted thirty years of his life to visiting the countless wonders of the world, wrote a two-volume work in which he described over 700 wonders—not just the classic seven. And he must have missed some, while others were not discovered until after his death.

The concept of a 'wonder of the world' has changed. Of course, even today one could limit oneself to the historic number of seven, as did the German newspaper *Die Welt* not long ago in an opinion poll of its readers from which the following list emerged: St Sophia in Istanbul, Golden Gate Bridge in San Francisco, the Acropolis in Athens, the Eiffel Tower in Paris, the Great Wall of China, the city of Brasilia, and the Taj Mahal in Agra. But any restricted list, com-piled on no rigid standard, must produce a distorted picture.

This book at least extends the limits. The world has become smaller; but the number of its wonders, especially in the field of technology, grows larger year by year. In this book sixty of the most remarkable, most beautiful, most magnificent sights in the world are picked out. Many people who knew well the subjects and countries in question collaborated in making the selection. The list was endlessly dis-cussed, expanded and pruned. And so a panorama of the wonders of the world was built up, ranging from the Egyptian pyramids to the blue-print metropolis of Brasilia, from Machu Picchu to the Niagara Falls, and from the Taj Mahal to Cape Kennedy. The choice of subjects may not be perfect, still less complete. Others would perhaps have chosen differently, but there never has been and never will be an ultimate canon of wonders of the world—for that the world is just too diverse and too transient, too beautiful, too strange—and too wonderful.

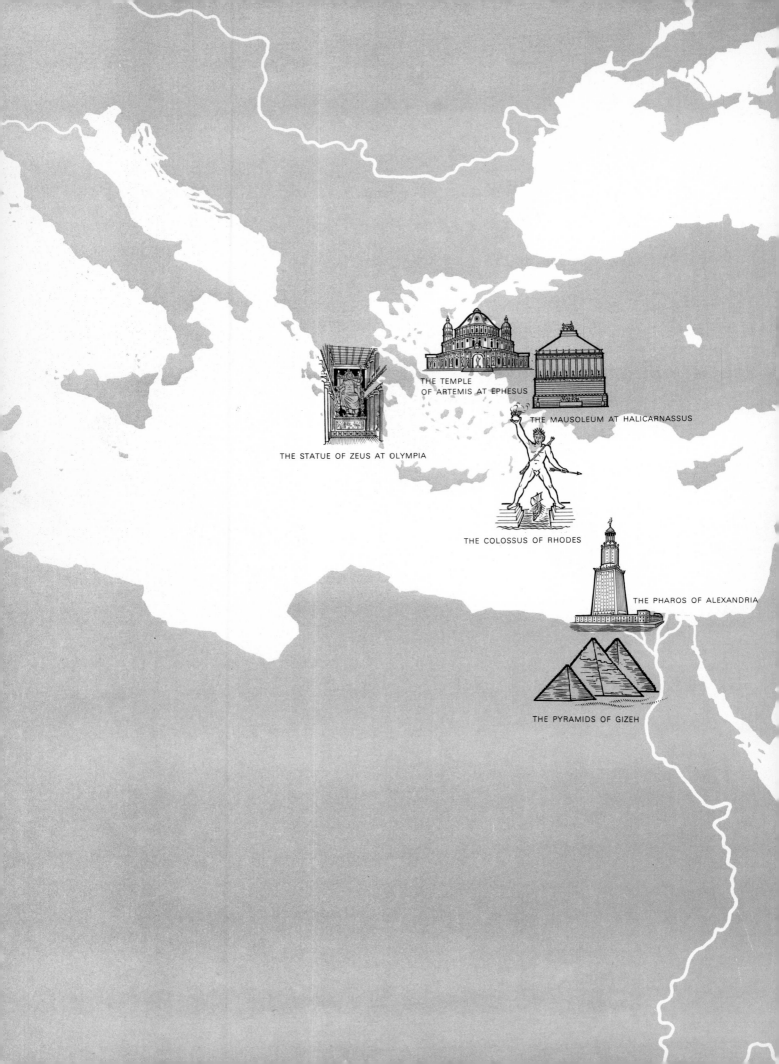

THE TEMPLE
OF ARTEMIS AT EPHESUS

THE MAUSOLEUM AT HALICARNASSUS

THE STATUE OF ZEUS AT OLYMPIA

THE COLOSSUS OF RHODES

THE PHAROS OF ALEXANDRIA

THE PYRAMIDS OF GIZEH

WONDERS OF ANTIQUITY

THE HANGING GARDENS

Before looking at the modern wonders of the world we should first remember the seven wonders of antiquity. Not that anyone is likely to have forgotten them. First were the Pyramids of Gizeh in Egypt, then the Hanging Gardens of Semiramis in Babylon, then . . . What else? It is really not so surprising that we have forgotten for, apart from the Egyptian pyramids, not one of the Classical wonders of the world can still be seen today. Six of the seven most famous buildings and sculptures of antiquity disappeared from the face of the earth long ago. No one knows what Phidias' statue of Zeus at Olympia or the Colossus of Rhodes even looked like. Their appearance can only be guessed at from incomplete sketches or stylized representations on coins. With the aid of historical documents reconstructions of the Temple of Artemis at Ephesus, the Mausoleum at Halicarnassus and the Pharos of Alexandria have been made, and they are probably something like the originals.

The first list of wonders of the world is thought to have been compiled by the Greek poet Antipater of Sidon between 150 and 120 BC. Why he wanted to draw up such a list we do not know, nor do we know whether Antipater had ever actually seen the buildings and sculptures he listed. All seven sights were chosen from a Greek point of view, but only one of them—the statue of Zeus by Phidias—stood on the soil of present-day Greece. Three of the wonders selected by the poet were to be seen in Asia Minor: the Colossus of Rhodes, the Temple of Artemis at Ephesus and the Mausoleum at Halicarnassus. A somewhat longer journey was necessary to see the pyramids of Gizeh, and the Hanging Gardens were a long way off, in Babylon. Wonders like the Acropolis in Athens, which were, in a manner of speaking, in his own backyard, Antipater left out. Others, such as the Tower of Babel, were not included because they were already in a state of dilapidation; Antipater was not interested in ruins. That there were precisely seven, and not thirteen or twenty wonders on his list, is probably connected in some way with the symbolic significance of the figure seven.

In later years more than a dozen notable buildings from all over the world were described as the 'eighth wonder of the world'. The first and most wildly imaginative reconstructions of the ancient wonders appeared in Europe with the revival of interest in the classical world. Marten de Vos (1532–1603) and the Jesuit Athanasius Kircher (1601–80), a German Jesuit scholar very famous during his lifetime, produced the first examples of this kind. Fischer von Erlach (1656–1723), the great Austrian architect, made a somewhat more realistic reconstruction. But not until modern archaeologists set to work did a reasonably accurate picture emerge.

The stone colossi of the Pharaohs

THE PYRAMIDS OF GIZEH

'Times defies everything, but the pyramids defy time,' says an Arab proverb. Over 4,500 years ago, some time during the hundred years between 2650 and 2550 BC, the three great pyramids of Gizeh were built, those of Cheops, Chephren and Mycerinos, three kings of the Fourth Dynasty of whom little is known other than that they commissioned their own pyramids.

Similarly, hardly anything is known about how the pyramids were built. The most detailed reports about their construction come from Herodotus, the 'Father of History'. In the year 450 BC he toured Egypt and learned from priests the amazing details which he handed down to posterity and which up to the present day have influenced our thinking. 'First of all a road was laid,' wrote Herodotus about the building of the pyramid of Cheops, 'along which the stones were brought to the Nile from the Libyan mountains.' This preparatory work lasted ten years. At the same time the burial chamber was carved out.

The actual pyramid, again according to Herodotus, was built in the space of twenty years. 100,000 people worked on the construction—but for a period of only three months every year, presumably at the time when the flooding of the Nile brought work in the fields to a halt. Ramps of loose stones, chutes, hoists and pulleys were used to transport over two million limestone blocks. 'The amount paid out for radishes, onions and garlic was recorded in Egyptian script on the pyramid and, if I remember rightly what the interpreter, who could read the script, told me, the cost was 1,600 talents,' wrote Herodotus. It is at this point in the report, if not sooner, that one becomes suspicious. It seems unlikely that the dragomen of Herodotus' time would be able to read hieroglyphics. But what do the other reports have to say? Paul Rieppel, who made an exhaustive study of the pyramids, the story of their construction and the numerical mysticism associated with them, worked out that, given a work force of 100,000 and a construction time of twenty times three months, even with the use of the simplest aids, the daily output of each individual could only be very meagre. The popular idea of slaves or forced labour bent under the whip begins to lose its credibility. Moreover, could such a crowd of workers be accommodated on the building site at all? Rieppel says not, and that 6,000 or at most 8,000 was the maximum. Perhaps they even managed with 4,000—there would hardly have been room for more in the large building which must once have stood near the pyramid of Cheops.

Thus the idea of the pyramids as a scene of wanton human exploitation begins gradually to change. It may be that the men of the construction gangs were pleased to be allowed to work on the sacred building. In any case the names of these men, preserved in the hieroglyphic script, testify to this conclusion.

Above: town of the dead west of the pyramids taken, like the photograph of the climbing Arab (centre) from the top of the pyramid of Cheops. Below: the pyramid of Cheops consists of stone blocks each weighing tons. Above left: the sphinx, 65 feet high and 242 feet long, keeps watch over the holy area of the pyramid of Chephren. Its foot (below right) gives an idea of its size. Far left: an impression of the pyramids in 1670.

Semiramis' flowering wonder

The Hanging Gardens

'Nebuchadnezzar ordered mounds of stone to be erected near his palace. They were to be made to look like mountains and were to be planted with all kinds of trees. At his wife's request he also had a garden set out of the kind common in her home country, Media.' The gardens described here by the Jewish writer Flavius Josephus (AD 37–100) are undoubtedly the famous Hanging Gardens of Semiramis'. However, Semiramis, described by the writers of antiquity as a woman possessing divine powers, was not Nebuchadnezzar's wife.

BABYLONIS MURI

Evidently it was not until later that the legendary figure of Semiramis, queen of Assyria, incidentally, and not of Babylon, was connected with the gardens of Nebuchadnezzar's wife, since there could no longer have been any doubt that the Babylonian king was responsible for having them built. When the German archaeologist Robert Koldewey started to excavate Babylon in 1899, he found in the north-eastern corner of the southern citadel a vaulted building with a deep well, exactly as described in the ancient reports. So far, Koldewey's conviction that what he had in front of him was the foundation of the Hanging Gardens has never been seriously challenged. Of course the gardens were never actually 'hanging'—this description could well have arisen from a mistranslation, for, although the Latin *penisilis* does mean 'hanging', it can also mean 'balcony-like'. The Gardens of Babylon bloomed on a terraced structure, a sort of roof garden, which could be watered artificially. It is easy to understand how the blossoming oasis in Babylon's desert climate caused a sensation (though it now seems strange that the famous Tower of Babel was not proclaimed a wonder of the world too). But by the time Alexander the Great came to Babylon the legendary tower was already in a state of decay and it was not until two hundred years later that the first list of wonders of the world appeared.

Brueghel's fantastic painting of the Tower of Babel (below) influenced the concept of this extraordinary building for many years. Like the three representations of the Hanging Gardens (left), it was painted about the middle of the sixteenth century. In the bottom left-hand picture (by Marten de Vos) the figure of Semiramis the huntress is portrayed against the background of her gardens.

Shrine of the goddess of fertility
The Temple of Artemis at Ephesus

The magnificent building in Ephesus dedicated to Artemis was described by Pliny as a temple 240 feet by 463 feet with 127 pillars, 36 of which were decorated with carvings. For a long time, however, Pliny's description was thought to be an exaggeration.

After a search lasting seven years, the English engineer, J. T. Wood found the site of the Temple of Ephesus where Ayasoluk now stands. This temple really must have been a wonder of t world, a building in which, according to Jacob Burckhardt, orie and occident had been mysteriously interwoven into a form unparalleled beauty. In 356 BC it was set on fire by a fanatic call Herostratus. Dinocrates had the temple rebuilt to the celebrat design on the old site. Finally, in AD 262, it was completely destroy by the Goths and what remained of the temple sank into t marshes.

Two historical but inaccurate reconstructions of the shrine Artemis (left). Above: statue of Artemis, the goddess of fertil worshipped in Ephesus, a different aspect of the deity better know to us as the chaste huntress of the Greeks.

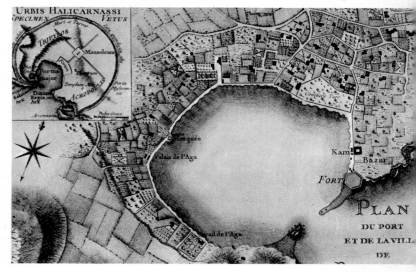

omb of the satrap

he Mausoleum at Halicarnassus

e wife of King Mausoleus, governor of the Persian province of
ria around 360 BC, ordered a tomb for her husband which was
proclaim his fame for ever.

t has not been possible to reconstruct the exact appearance of
Mausoleum. In the fourteenth century the knights of the Order
St John used the tomb as a quarry for the building of the citadel

of Peter at Halicarnassus (now called Bodrum). In doing so, they
cleared it away so thoroughly that only the chiselled-out rock was
left to show where the famous building had once stood. The tomb,
with an area of 108 feet by 128 feet, stood almost 165 feet high
and must have been visible for miles. Five platforms supported a
wall reaching to half the total height, and on this stood the actual
tomb surrounded by columns and covered by a pyramidal roof
which was crowned by an enormous quadriga.

**The reconstruction by Mothes (top) may well be close to the true
appearance of the Mausoleum. The nineteenth-century engraving,
on the other hand, is probably a somewhat distorted representation
(above left). Right: an old map of Halicarnassus.**

Gigantic statue of the sun god
The Colossus of Rhodes

According to a contemporary writer, there were in ancient Rhodes, at that time an island of considerable wealth, 3,000 statues, a hundred of which were of immense proportions. Among these was the most famous giant statue of antiquity, the Colossus of Rhodes, which was reputedly between 100 to 130 feet high and is supposed to have weighed 70 tons. This bronze figure depicting the sun god Helios with a burning torch in his outstretched hand is said to have stood on two enormous stone pedestals astride the entrance to Rhodes harbour.

Tradition has it that the people of Rhodes decided to build the statue of the god who protected them after their victory in the fourth century BC over Demetrius Poliorcetes, king of Macedonia, who after a long but unsuccessful siege on the island had eventually been forced to withdraw. It is said that the islanders sold the arms and implements left behind by the retreating army and used the proceeds for the statue.

The sculptor Chares was entrusted with the work and in 291 drew up the first designs. Twelve years later the enormous project was completed. It had only been standing for just over 50 years when an earthquake which shook Rhodes toppled it into the sea, leaving nothing but parts of the enormous feet on the pedestals.

In AD 653 the remains of the statue were sold by the occupying Saracens to a Jewish merchant who divided them into 900 camel loads and transported them to the mainland where they were melted down and probably made into weapons. Nobody knows exactly what the Colossus of Rhodes looked like but 'at all events the sight must have been indescribably hideous, tasteless, offensive, moreover indecent on a quite intolerable scale', as Willy Haas critically remarked when he heard about the plans to have the Colossus reconstructed in the interests of tourism.

No authentic drawings of the Colossus of Rhodes, the giant statue of the sun god Helios, have been handed down, and so artists could let their imagination run free (above and right). It is not even known whether the bronze sculpture really did stand astride the entrance to the harbour.

Sostratus' beacon

The Pharos of Alexandria

The lighthouse at Alexandria is considered one of the greatest technical achievements of antiquity. Designed by the Greek architect Sostratus, who came from Knidos, it was built about 300 to 280 BC on a peninsula overlooking the Egyptian port. It consisted of a broad rectangular base with a narrower octagonal superstructure over 300 feet high. At night a fire of wood and pitch was lit on the uppermost platform.

Legend has it that Sostratus searched for a long time to find a material resistant to sea water for the foundations before finally building his tower on enormous blocks of glass. The beacon, called Pharos after the peninsula on which it stood, was finally destroyed by an earthquake in 1375, but its name remains even though the ruins have never been found.

The Statue of Zeus at Olympia

Very little is known about the actual appearance of the statue of Zeus which stood in the temple built in 456 BC at Olympia. The representation of the god, carved out of ivory and ebony and richly decorated with gold and precious stones, is said to have been 50 feet high. The Greeks considered it a personal misfortune not to have seen this national shrine. 'The sight of Zeus would move even an insensible creature' (Chrysostomos).

The statue of Zeus was the last work of the Greek sculptor Phidias, one of whose earlier works, built in the same style, was the statue of Athena Parthenos on the Acropolis. He depicted the most important of the Greek gods with a wrinkled forehead for, according to Greek beliefs, Olympus shook whenever Zeus wrinkled his brow.

Three attempts to depict the Pharos at Alexandria (top and second row) and an old map of Alexandria with the lighthouse. Third row: did the temple of Zeus with the golden statue of the god look like this? Bottom: reconstruction of Olympia (nineteenth-century) – in the middle the enormous temple of Zeus.

THINGVELLIR

SURTSEY

HOLLAND'S DELTA PLAN

STONEHENGE

LA RANCE TIDAL POWER STATION

COLOGNE CATHEDRAL

THE ATOMIUM

ARC DE TRIOMPHE

THE EIFFEL TOWER

VERSAILLES

RONCHAMP

GLOCKNER-KAPRUN

THE MONT BLANC TUNNEL

MILAN CATHEDRAL

POSTOJNA CAVES

VENICE

THE ESCORIAL

ST PETER'S IN ROME

ANCIENT ROME

VESUVIUS

THE ALHAMBRA

THE KREMLIN

WONDERS OF EUROPE

Over 2,000 years ago when the Greek poet Antipater compiled his first list of wonders of the world, he overlooked the architectural and sculptural art of Greece, except in one instance, the statue of Zeus by Phidias in the temple at Olympia. The Acropolis in Athens, today the source of boundless admiration, was not included on the list. Was it too near his own doorstep? Willy Haas once observed in ironic vein: 'Today one would say the whole thing is typical of the publicity of a tourist agency which does not cater for short excursions because they would not be profitable enough.' As this book was compiled in Europe (even if assistants, especially photographers, from all parts of the world collaborated on it), there was a danger that it too might tend to neglect the wonders on the doorstep. This thought brings us to an apparently typical phenomenon concerning wonders of the world. The foreign visitor sees things with different eyes: he may be unimpressed by what swells the breast of the local inhabitants with pride. In foreign countries one automatically tends to admire anything which does not occur in the same form in one's own country. The inhabitants, on the other hand, have grown accustomed to their surroundings: one cannot remain in a perpetual state of amazement. As Goethe said: 'The greatest wonder is that wonders become so commonplace to us.' To recognise the wonderful, we must have a capacity for wonder.

Almost everywhere in Europe one finds things to admire. As well as the achievements of architecture, there are those of modern technology and the wonders of nature. If one takes these three fields as the basis for one's selection, as in this book, Europe perhaps outranks other continents in sheer diversity.

With such a wide field to choose from, it was particularly difficult to make a selection. Sometimes it was a neck-and-neck race. Were Chartres Cathedral and Strasbourg not worth considering? What about the Tower of London and the Hradčany Castle in Prague, the Lion Gate at Mycenae, the Corinth Canal, the Benedictine Abbey of Monte Cassino, the Leaning Tower of Pisa, Heidelberg Castle?

Some may feel that the Soviet Union has been treated rather poorly. That is unfortunately true, but inevitable as it was not possible to obtain from Russia actual plans of technical projects or even permission to send a photographer to some parts of the Soviet Union.

THE ACROPOLIS

Germany's largest church

COLOGNE CATHEDRAL

There are several reasons why Cologne Cathedral, the largest cathedral in Germany and one of the most important churches in the world, excites such admiration. To begin with its overwhelming dimensions almost exceed the bounds of the imagination: the towers are 515 feet high; the inside area is 472 feet long and almost 145 feet wide; and the vault of the nave is over 140 feet high. Secondly, the unsurpassed harmony of its parts is admirable; and finally the unity of the Gothic order which gives it the effect of sheer weightlessness is extraordinary. When the foundation stone was laid in 1248, during the office of Archbishop Konrad of Hochstaden, Cologne already had a history dating back 1,300 years. In about 50 BC a Roman colony was founded on the site, the Colonia Claudia Ara Agrippinensium. Colonia became Cöllen and then Köln (Cologne). Close to the cathedral the remains of a Roman palace were found with the Dionysus mosaic dating from the second century AD and measuring 807 square feet. In 1959 two regally furnished Frankish graves dating from the middle of the sixth century were discovered deep in the ground under the cathedral choir.

At the beginning of the ninth century Archbishop Hildebold, chaplain to Charlemagne, built a double-choired basilica, the 'Old Cathedral'. The prestige of this precursor of the present cathedral was heightened when in 1164 the supposed relics of the Three Wise Men were conveyed by Archbishop Rainald of Dassel, chancellor to the Emperor Barbarossa, from Milan to Cologne. Through these relics the new cathedral acquired the stature of a royal church, connected with Christ as the greatest king. The significance of this is demonstrated by the fact that during the Middle Ages it was the Archbishop of Cologne who crowned the German kings at Aachen and that the first two seats in the choir stalls in Cologne Cathedral were always reserved for the emperor and the pope.

The building commenced in 1248 advanced very hesitantly. The choir was finished by 1320 and consecrated in 1322. Two storeys of the south tower were not completed until 1400; during the fourteenth, fifteenth and sixteenth centuries the nave and transept were built to a height of 49 feet and 59 feet, respectively. At that point everything came to a halt until the nineteenth century. Of the enormous shell the only part used for services was the choir, and for a long time it looked as though the building would never be completed. A pamphlet published in 1880 to commemorate the completion of the cathedral says: 'Gradually all sense and understanding of the building style of the Middle Ages was lost. It would have been considered an offence against the spirit of the time to try to complete the ruins of the cathedral in the old style.'

There were repeated demands that the building of the cathedral should be resumed. As someone pointed out: 'If the nave, the colossal towers and the remaining parts of the building were finished, Europe would have nothing greater to show; it could be compared with the ancient wonders of the world.'

It was not just a question of money but also of the difference in attitude: 'When Gothic was sacrificed to the new spirit of the times Cologne, too, submitted to the union of Rococo and pedantry. People tried to outdo each other in pasting over, planing off and mutilating the existing works of art.'

Eventually the crucial impetus to get the final stages of building under way came from S. Boiserée who managed to interest Goethe in it. During the period from 1842 to 1880 the missing limbs were added to the enormous body 'in the spirit of the past'. New and old were joined without discord. Only the sculptures lacked the powerful expressiveness which is a unique feature of the art of the Middle Ages.

Soon Cologne Cathedral came to be regarded as a symbol of Germany, but its true significance lies elsewhere. The ethereal quality imparted to the stone by the diffusion of light through the coloured windows is to be perceived as an image of the Cathedral of Heaven. The building, in spite of its monumental structure, gives an impression of weightlessness. To appreciate this fully one must bear in mind that a single coping stone in the central aisle, for example, weighs almost two tons. This should be borne in mind when one considers the stupendous task that faced the restorers after the end of the Second World War.

Many books have been written about the art treasures of the cathedral, but the Gero cross dating from about 970, possibly the oldest sculptural representation of the crucifix in existence, should be mentioned. The shrine of the Three Kings is internationally famous. The largest piece of goldsmith's work in the world, it was started in 1181 by Nicolas of Verdun and completed around 1220 by craftsmen in Cologne. The statues of the apostles on the pillars of the chancel are considered the most important sculptures of fourteenth century Germany. No less remarkable are the medieval windows and the brilliant workmanship of the sacristy. The triptych by Stephen Lochner is regarded as the masterpiece of the fifteenth century Cologne school of painting.

Among other damage, the arches in the central aisle and nothern transept were destroyed during the Second World War. For eleven years seventy workmen were engaged in rectifying the damage to the cathedral. They kept strictly to the original plans, and today Cologne Cathedral is once again a complete and perfect whole, a striking landmark visible for miles.

The shrine of the Three Kings (above left) is one of the cathedral's most valuable art treasures. Above right: southern gate with the door by Mataré. For hundreds of years the half-finished cathedral stood like a headless trunk (centre: engraving from the year 1531). Bottom left: one of the pinnacles designed for the towers of the cathedral. Bottom right: the cruciform plan of Cologne Cathedral. Far right: nave and choir of the cathedral.

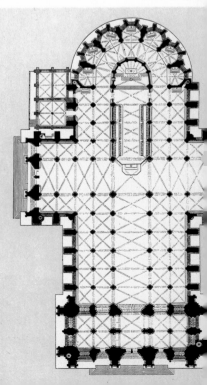

The dam system in the Grossglockner region is Austria's largest source of hydro-electric power, but for a long time neither the 6,000 million cubic feet of water stored in three dams (Margaritze, Wasserfall and Moserboden), nor the power station's output of 200,000 kilowatts have, by international standards, seemed very impressive. Nevertheless, the world took note when the first reports about the Kaprun project were made known. It was difficult to know which to admire more—the courage with which the Austrians set about building dam walls up to 400 feet high in the lofty, virtually unexplored mountains under the most difficult climatic and technological conditions, or their determination to harness and utilize as fully as possible their relatively meagre water supplies. The 7½-mile-long Kaprun Valley is 4,000 feet deep, and a complicated system of roads, cable railways, hoists and cable cranes had to be set up to transport personnel, materials and machinery. The task of construction in the high mountains (concreting, for instance, was possible on only 150 days of the year) proved to be a dramatic and hazardous venture. Avalanches, landslides and unpredictable changes in the weather often made life sheer hell for the workmen, but they carried on. Today there is no trace of the difficulties that beset them and Kaprun has long since become accepted as very

much more than just a feature of the landscape. It is an engineering achievement of which the Austrians are justifiably proud.

Right: the 6¼ mile long Pasterze glacier lies at the foot of the 12,460 foot Grossglockner summit (left in picture). Its water is channelled into the Margaritze reservoir. Above: the Moserboden reservoir of the Glockner-Kaprun group.

24

ower station in the high Alps

LOCKNER–KAPRUN

The organizers of the World Exhibition in Brussels in 1958 dreamt of a building that, as the focal point of the world exhibition, would be 'a symbol for the whole of mankind'. The engineer and business manager, André Waterkeyn came up with an astonishing suggestion: he proposed that an authentic reconstruction of the nine atoms of an alpha iron crystal, built on a scale of 1:150,000,000,000, should tower over the exhibition site in the grounds of Laeken Palace. 'For what,' he said in support of his proposition, 'more clearly represents progress in the eyes of mankind than the splitting of the atom?' The jury was full of enthusiasm. Known as the Atomium, Waterkeyn's 348-foot-high construction of steel and aluminium became the sensation of an exhibition abounding in architectural surprises. By the time Expo '58 closed its doors, the nine silvery atom balls had become Brussels' new landmark, even replacing its 'oldest citizen', the Manneken Pis, on posters published by the Belgian Tourist Board. They can be seen miles away and seem to float weightlessly above the Belgian capital. Their high polish is due to a 2-mm-thick layer of aluminium which was applied by electrolysis. After dark, countless bulbs outline their contours. The Atomium not only has an arresting exterior but also an inner life full of interest. Each of the nine glittering spheres measures 65 feet in diameter. Up five escalators (including, the Belgians claim, the longest one in Europe) and several flights of stairs, one passes through the 10-foot-wide connecting tubes into the lateral globes containing a snack bar and permanent exhibition illustrating the peaceful uses of atomic energy. A lift carries the visitor at a speed of 16 feet per second to the main attraction of the Atomium, the cosy circular restaurant in the highest globe, from which one can enjoy an excellent view of the city over a glass of Belgian beer or a dish of Brussels poulard.

The Atomium, Brussels' landmark, towers 348 feet above the Belgian capital (far right). The view at night is enchanting (above). The base of the Atomium (right) gives some idea of its enormous proportions.

Symbol of the atomic age
THE ATOMIUM

Holland's fight against the sea

HOLLAND'S DELTA PLAN

A plaque in the arrival lounge of Schiphol, Amsterdam's airport, announces 'Altitude: 13 feet below sea level'. Almost half the Netherlands lies below mean sea level, and for 1,200 years the Dutch have been waging a bitter struggle against the sea. Dykes and sandbanks, stretching for 1,120 miles, protect the land, and for seventy-five years work has been going on to partition off and partially drain the Zuider Zee.

The south-western coastal area with its many islands and peninsulas and enormous river deltas encompassing the outlets of the Rhine, the Schelde and the Maas, has always been particularly prone to flooding. When, during the catastrophe of February 1953, thousands of acres of fertile land were flooded as a result of numerous breaks in the dykes, the government produced plans to reduce the coastline of the delta area by over 1,100 miles. As well as some smaller dams, the scheme provides for the damming up of four broad deep inlets, though two waterways to the harbours of Rotterdam and Amsterdam are to remain open. The project is intended to be finished within twenty years and will cost about £100,000,000.

Work on the colossal scheme was commenced as quickly as possible. Enormous building sites appeared simultaneously in several places. In 1960–1, under the provisions of the Three Island Plan, the islands of Walcheren and North and South Beveland were linked by enormous dams, and in 1964 the Grevelingen dam between Overflakkee and Duiveland was completed.

The Haringvliet dam is also operating. It is equipped with a system of seventeen double locks, each one weighing 425 tons and opening on a width of over 185 feet.

And almost as an incidental two more bridges appeared—one over the Haringvliet, the other more than three miles long, over the Oosterschelde, which at present holds the record as the longest bridge in Europe.

Above: with the help of enormous caissons, a new dam is sectioned off. Centre: the extensive lock system of the Haringvliet dam. Bottom: Oosterschelde Bridge. Far left: the Grevelingen dam between the islands of Overflakkee and Duiveland.
Pages 28–29: the three-mile long Oosterschelde Bridge, Europe's longest bridge, photographed from North Beveland.

31

THE ESCORIAL

Some people find it cold, gloomy, forbidding; others, monumental and majestic. This enormous building, a mixture of palace, monastery and mausoleum, set in the solitude of the granite mountains of the Sierra de Guadarrama, was built at the command of Philip II. It took 30 years to construct at a cost of 5,260,570 ducats, and since its completion the tongues of the critics have never been still. Some historians accuse the designers of wanton extravagance and a style of building geared to Spanish court etiquette. To the Spaniards the *Real Monasterio de San Lorenzo* — that is its official name — is *the* Spanish building, just as Cervantes' *Don Quixote* is *the* Spanish novel.

Present-day art historians are less critical in their judgement of the monastery cum palace, with its 16 courtyards, 2,673 windows, 1,200 doors, 86 flights of stairs, 88 fountains and passages providing a 100-mile march. For them the plain austere style of the Escorial is like a greeting over the centuries. The style is known as *Estilo Herreresco*, Herrera style. Juan de Herrera (about 1530–97) was Philip II's architect. He completed what his teacher, Juan Bautista de Toledo, had begun in 1563.

When Philip II decided to have a monumental palace built in the solitude of the mountains, Madrid had not become the official capital of Spain. On 10 August 1557, the feast day of St Lawrence, Philip had defeated the French near St Quentin. The Escorial was to be a monument to this victory, its grid-shaped ground-plan symbolizing the gridiron on which St Lawrence suffered a martyr's death.

Toledo and Herrera arranged the buildings ordered by the king for the palace enclosure in a rectangle 226 yards long and 176 yards wide with a tower at each corner. A monastery, an enormous church modelled on St Peter's in Rome, a royal palace, in which Philip II required for himself just one small room where he could rest his weary limbs, and eventually a museum, a library and the *Pantoon de los Reyes* with the tombs of the Spanish kings were built. Philip II had the body of his father and great exemplar, the Emperor Charles V, interred in the crypt under the church. The space beside the dead emperor was left vacant: an inscription near the grave announces: 'If a descendant of Charles V should surpass him in the boldness of his deeds, then he may occupy this place.' Today the space is still unoccupied: Philip II did not claim it. Certainly, his reign was not as brilliant as his father's — one only has to think of the destruction of the Armada, the revolt of the Netherlands and the bankruptcy of the royal treasury. The king died in one of the oratories in his church, his gaze fixed on the high altar.

The austere style of the palace was not to the liking of his successors, who 'improved' it in the style of the seventeenth and eighteenth centuries, but the 'rubbish dump' (that is the literal translation of *Escorial*) was not basically changed. Today the enormous building still lies brooding in the bleak landscape, a granite block in granite mountains.

In the opinion of Franz Litschauer, 'The Escorial belongs to the most powerful aesthetic effects in the world, to the greatest palace buildings in the history of art.'

The grid-shaped ground-plan of the palace shows up clearly in this bird's-eye view (below right) from a print, 1587. The pinnacle of the dome (centre) stands 312 feet above the floor of the church which was modelled on St Peter's in Rome. Above: floodlights add enchantment to the austere building – the Escorial as tourists see it. Far right above: the Escorial with the Sierra de Guadarrama in the distance. Below: the 'Antesala de Embajadores', the 'anteroom of the ambassadors'.

Pages 30–31: the south façade of the Escorial.

A Moorish castle above Granada
THE ALHAMBRA

The inhabitants of Granada have always maintained 'Anyone who has not seen Granada has not seen anything.' Alexandre Dumas went even further in his praise: 'God created the Alhambra and Granada in case one day he should grow tired of his own home.' As a 'dream become reality' set in a 'landscape kissed by the sun' other poets have eulogized the 'pearl of Andalusia'.

To anyone who has seen the Alhambra this rapture is understandable. Even from the outside the impact of this, the most famous example of Islamic architecture in Europe and a symbol of former power and glory, is felt through the grandeur of its red walls and towers. The Moors called the palace, *Kalat al-hambra*, the red fortress, but its interior walls look as if they are made of Brussels lace.

Granada, now a city with almost 160,000 inhabitants and the capital of Upper Andalusia, first attained real significance after the beginning of the Arab rule in Spain (AD 711). In 1031 it became the capital of an autonomous kingdom, and during the centuries that followed developed into a centre of Moorish culture, art and learning. The founding of the Alhambra occurred during the heyday of the Granada kingdom. Under Mohammed I (1232–72), the first ruler of the Nasrides dynasty, work started on the building of a royal castle on the Monte de la Asabica. By this time the *Reconquista*, the reconquest of Spain by the Christian kings of the north, was well under way, and the sphere of Moorish influence was becoming smaller and smaller. When Mohammed V (1354–91) finally ordered the construction of the splendid buildings of the Alhambra, Granada was already the last remaining outpost of Moorish dominion in Spain.

A hundred years after the death of Mohammed V the Catholic kings of Aragon and Castile seized Granada and occupied the Alhambra. Legend has it that Boabdil, the last Moorish ruler in Spain, wept when he left his castle through the Puerta de los Siete Suelos and requested that this gate to the palace of palaces should be sealed for ever. During the flight across the Sierra Nevada, the story goes on, Boabdil once again turned with tear-filled eyes to take a last look at Granada (the place is still called *El Suspiro del Moro*, the sigh of the Moor), and was taunted by his mother Aisha because of his lack of courage: 'Do not cry like a woman because you did not choose to fight like a man!'

Even after the withdrawal of the Moors, Granada retained its Moorish appearance. To commemorate their victory, the conquerors had a cathedral built, in which the *muertos immortales* (immortal dead), Ferdinand and Isabella, the Catholic kings were later buried. The flags of Aragon and Castile bearing the Christian cross flew above the Alhambra and the magnificent building soon began to

The Lion Courtyard was once the centre of the royal winter residence. Its name is derived from the lion fountain, the 'Fuente de los Leones'.

fall into decay. Later the rooms of the Alhambra became a refuge for vagabonds and gypsies. During the Napoleonic Wars, Wellington had some of the rooms renovated, but in 1812 part of the fortress was blown up by the French. Then in the nineteenth century the decaying treasures were remembered and the work of restoration began.

Today the tourist sees the Alhambra completely restored to its former beauty. He admires the Arab garden at the foot of the palace precincts, visits the citadel (Alcazaba) with its enormous walls and terraces, compares Charles V's palace (a Renaissance building never completed) with the Moorish buildings and goes on an excursion to the Palacio del Generalife, the summer seat of the Moorish kings, originally established as Dshennat al-Arif, Garden of Arif, with its beautiful public gardens. They are famous in Spanish song.

All these remarkable buildings and gardens, however, pale in comparison with the fairy-tale splendour of the actual palace of Alhambra (*Palacio arabe*). The outside, as of all Moorish secular buildings, is not particularly striking, which makes the interior all the more impressive. Well-known are the two large courtyards—the Myrtle Courtyard with its recesses and colonnades, and the Lion Courtyard with the fountain whose basin is supported by twelve black marble lions. In the Comares Tower lies the Ambassador Chamber, once the state room of the kings, in which Boabdil gathered his counsellors round him for the last time before the surrender of Granada.

Other features of interest are the underground baths, with separate [baths] for children and women as well as Turkish baths; the Queen's [b]udoir built on the steep cliff face; the Abencerrajes Room in [wh]ich, according to legend, several members of the Abencerrajes [fam]ily were beheaded because of a love affair between the head [of t]he family, Hamet, and Boabdil's wife.

[M]ost impressive of all is the varied style of interior ornamentation, [wit]h ceilings and arches arranged in such a way that they resemble [lime]stone caves, and walls dotted with Arabic inscriptions. Kurt [T]scher once admitted 'Music is really the only language capable [of pr]operly describing such beauty, which, like Persian carpets and [cas]hmere shawls, covers the walls in a blaze of colour, as if a rain-[bo]w had fallen out of the sky and poured itself over them.' The

builders themselves were not slow to praise: one of the Arabic inscriptions on the walls of the Alhambra says 'Allah has over-whelmed me with such a wealth of beauty that even the stars in the sky fettered in their path stand still and look down on me.'

The elegant Myrtle Courtyard (below left) is dominated by the silhouette of the Comares Tower. The Sala de los Reyes (Chamber of the Kings) is reached through ornate archways (right). Bottom row, left to right: detail of the Lion Fountain; Tower of the Ladies with garden; detail from the Chamber of the Kings. Far left: view from the Sierra Nevada of the towers and walls of the Alhambra.

The dying city
VENICE

More has been written about Venice than almost any other city in the world. In 1364 Petrarch found it 'rich in gold but richer still in glory'; in 1786 Goethe thought it beyond comparison with any other city; in 1798 Ernst Moritz Arndt was upset by 'disgusting sights and smells'; in 1844 Charles Dickens enthused over the reality of Venice that surpassed 'the imagination of the wildest dream' and in 1913 Thomas Mann called Venice 'the most unlikely of cities'.

The beginnings of the city, built on the 117 islands and islets in the lagoon separated from the sea by a sandbank, the Lido, date back to the fifth century AD. At that time the inhabitants of Aquilegia, who had been harassed by the Huns, took refuge on some of the marshy islands. The place of refuge grew into a commercial metropolis which dominated the sea. It was consecrated to St Mark in 827 when the bones of the apostle were brought to Venice from Alexandria. By 1204 it had achieved such power that the doge, Enrico Dandolo, ruled Constantinople for some years after its capture by the Crusaders.

In the fifteenth century Venice, with over 200,000 inhabitants, was the centre of world trade and the largest seaport in the world. The splendid buildings, reminiscent of oriental originals, became even more splendid. New palaces arose richly decorated by artists like Tintoretto and Veronese, Titian and Giorgione. The city, with its 150 canals and 400 bridges had reached its peak. The decline started when the Turks took Constantinople from the Venetians in the late fifteenth century. Much more damaging was the discovery by the Portuguese of the sea route to India. Overnight, pepper could be bought in Lisbon for a fifth of the price charged in Venice. Trade links were eroded, power and wealth diminished and Venice became a declining city.

In essence Venice today still looks the same as it did in its heyday. In the eyes of many tourists, Venice is a stone relic that everyone should see. Apart from St Mark's Square with its splendid 575-foot-long pavement, St Mark's church with its decorative pillars and mosaics and the free-standing 324-foot-high Campanile, and the impressive Doge's Palace with its arcades of pointed arches, one of the greatest attractions is the canal system. The two-mile-long Grand Canal which winds through the town in a broad S-shape, and even now a romantic ride in a gondola on the Grand Canal is on the programme of every visitor to Venice, although the 400 gondolas (in 1750 there were over 12,000) have long been in a hopeless minority among the hordes of motor boats.

Theodore Fontane, who visited Venice in 1874, found the city on one hand magical and poetic, but at the same time dirty—like a beautiful girl with an unwashed neck. 'It needs moonlight so that it can be only half seen,' he remarked. Unfortunately, all the splendour of the past cannot alter the fact that Venice is, not only historically but also physically, a dying city. The palazzi built on marshy land with a timber raft or wooden piles as a foundation are gradually sinking into the lagoon. Many of them, especially the privately owned houses, are in a lamentable state. The lagoon is silting up and the population is falling. Despite world-wide efforts, there are grave doubts whether Venice has any future at all. That this would be a tragedy goes without saying. Venice is unique—an exquisite city that was founded in necessity and made its way to glory. But it is bound to lose in its struggle to survive in an age of machines. The very charm that no other city can rival has brought tourists by the million and the machines that aid their arrival contribute to the city's doom. The motor boats that replace the gondolas can be seen to saturate the stone of the buildings as they race by—and they are only a single factor. It is often said that Venice *must* be saved. A way to save it has yet to be found.

Above: clocktower in St Mark's Square; in the foreground one of the bronze horses of San Marco. Centre: the Doge's Palace. Below: St Mark's Square and harbour in the fifteenth century. Far right: Rialto Bridge (above left). St Mark's church (below) and regatta on the Grand Canal (right). Below: aerial photograph of the centre of Venice. Pages 40-41: the enchantment of Venice at twilight.

Gothic architecture south of the Alps
MILAN CATHEDRAL

A perplexing filigree of turrets and towers, spires and pinnacles, colonnades and statues embellishes the white marble splendour of Milan Cathedral which, after St Peter's in Rome, is the second largest church in Europe. There is room for 40,000 people in the nave which has an area of 13,993 square yards — almost twice that of Cologne Cathedral. The cross-shaped basilica was modelled on Gothic principles and is the largest Gothic building south of the Alps. However, in the context of the broad cathedral square with its palatial buildings, it looks remarkably 'un-Gothic'.

Jacob Burckhardt once called the cathedral a 'disastrous compromise between the Italian style and a sudden belated enthusiasm for the brilliant effects of northern detail. In essence,' he continued, 'the façade is Italian — to be exact, Lombard — and all the pinnacles cannot disguise its broad character. Italian, too, is the relatively small difference in height between the central and the outer aisles. As to the rest, the most unfortunate excesses and deficiences of the northern embellishments predominate.'

The dual impression it made on this famous critic can be explained by the history of the cathedral's construction, which extended over six centuries from the time when it was initiated by the first duke of Milan, Giovanni Galeazzo Visconti, a man with a taste for the magnificent. At the side of the Italian architects he placed French and German advisers, but his choice of architects was evidently unfortunate, for they constantly quarrelled and as a result progress on the work suffered. It was not until 150 years after work on the building had started that the dome could be constructed, and a further sixty years passed before the crypt, baptistery and marble floor were finished. The façade was tackled at a leisurely pace and was not finished until the beginning of the nineteenth century with the result that Baroque and neo-Gothic influences became mixed.

In appreciation of the substantial contribution made by Napoleon towards the tower above the dome a stone bust of him was carved and superimposed on one of the 2,300 statues of saints on the front. In the opinion of the Milanese, however, the tower was a poor substitute for a proper campanile. It was generally agreed that it was only fitting for a cathedral as impressive as Milan's to have a campanile of suitable proportions. In 1938 the architect, Vico Vigano worked out an acceptable design for a free-standing tower in the Gothic style. With a height of 538 feet it was to be 10 feet taller than the highest church tower in the world, the 528 foot tower of Ulm Minster. The paper *Corriere della Sera* said, 'In its conception and proportions the tower will prove to be worthy of fascist Milan,' for there was not the slightest intention of using the tower for religious purposes. Mussolini, who had submitted the project to Vigano, wanted to make the campanile a grandiose dedication to fascist Italy. The Duce envisaged rooms with mosaics of battles, victory statues, an 'altar of the Fatherland' and a gallery of famous Milanese. He ordered the project to be completed by 1942.

Fortunately, because of the war, nothing came of this grandiose plan. It never got beyond the slender little tower which stands 130 feet higher than the dome and whose tip bears a gilded statue of the Virgin Mary. The Milanese call her affectionately *Madonnina*, little Madonna. It is possible to climb right up to the highest balcony on

the tower: there are 370 steps from the Cathedral Square. By the magnificent church was basically complete. Only the five doors were missing—and again there was no rush to get them In 1906 the sculptor Lodovico Poghliaghi designed the first in the contemporary style but it is questionable whether this suitable for the Gothic building. Two further doors follow 1948 and 1950, but it was not until 1965 that the last one finished. Luciano Minguzzi, a sculptor from Bologna, sugges door divided into fourteen scenes, each depicting an event the cathedral's history. The first shows the Milanese Archb Antonio de Saluzza studying Pope Urban II's letter of approv the plan to build the cathedral.

After the last door had been put in place, Milan Cathedra

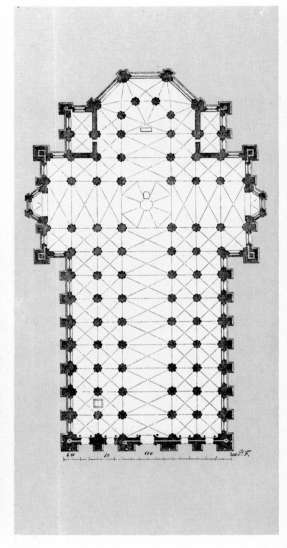

emnly declared complete—579 years after building had started.
Christian church, no heathen temple, no mosque can match
curious splendour of Milan Cathedral,' wrote Ernst von Hesse-
rtegg, and he added rather ruefully. 'The splendour of the marble
use of God is to great that it overshadows everything else worthy
admiration in big, beautiful Milan and its surroundings.'

t-hand page: figures of saints on the turrets (left above); ela-
ate decoration on the façade (left below). Centre above: ground
n of the cathedral. Centre below: head of the Madonna on top
the tower. Right: design for the cathedral's campanile drawn up
938 – it was passed by Mussolini but never built. Below: view
ough the buttressing and towers of the cathedral.

In the first century BC, the Roman scholar Varro fixed the date on which Rome was founded. It was, he decided, on 2 April 753 BC (in our calendar) that the twin brothers Romulus and Remus founded the city on the Tiber, but later researchers came to the conclusion that there could not have been any organized settlement in the vicinity of the Seven Hills of Rome until much later. However, a few years ago a new excavation was undertaken on the rubble of the Forum in the heart of the city precincts of ancient Rome, and it was then confirmed that Rome actually had been populated and built in the eighth century BC.

Today, the Forum Romanum, situated between the Capitoline, Palatine and Esquiline hills, is the most extensive site of ancient ruins in Rome and one of the most imposing in the world. For about 1,000 years it served the Romans as market- and meeting-place and seat of justice.

Over the long, troubled centuries its appearance continually changed, for it was the desire of every self-respecting Roman ruler to immortalize himself by constructing an impressive building in the Forum. Basilicas and temples, triumphal arches and monuments were built in honour of Julius Caesar, Augustus, Vespasian, Antoninus, Faustina, Tiberius, Titus, Severus and others. Shrines were erected to Janus, Saturn, Castor, Vesta, Venus, Roma and Romulus. Once an open market place, it eventually became so full of grand marble buildings decked with gold that little of the originally spacious design could be discerned, and the emperors moved to the seclusion of other squares.

During the sixth century the monuments and temples in the Roman Forum began to deteriorate. Some were made into Christian churches, some were used as quarries; sometimes the costly marble was burned to produce quicklime. Eventually the rubble piled up to a height of 43 feet over the ancient paving. When at last in the nineteenth century it was decided to excavate the centre of ancient Rome, the large area was being used as a *Campo vaccino* where cows grazed.

A similar fate also befell the Amphitheatreum Flavium, Rome's most prominent building of the imperial era, which stood near the Forum. For a thousand years or so it has been known as the Colosseum after a colossal statue of Nero which stood nearby. The enormous building, with about 50,000 seats then, as today, the largest theatre in the world, was completed in the year AD 80. During the opening festivities, which lasted a hundred days, 5,000 wild animals were killed by the gladiators. Mass battles, war scenes, animal baiting, whole sea battles and finally the public torture and execution of tens of thousands of Christians were staged in the Colosseum for the enjoyment of the people. 'There was hardly a torture known from history or literature, or dreadful way of death, with whose performance the people in the amphitheatre were not entertained.' (Ludwig Friedländer).

The four-storey elliptical building (205 yards long and 170 yards wide), which could be covered with canvas against sun or rain, was the centre for the Roman gladiator spectacles for 400 years. Until the year 1000 the walls were left untouched, for the Romans believed the superstition that if the Colosseum fell Rome too would fall. But then the building was used as a quarry and by the time the plundering was brought to a halt only a ruin was left. Yet even now it still gives an impression of the power and greatness of ancient Rome.

Much visited by tourists, the Forum has more to offer than an absorbing excursion into Rome's imperial past. It is an extremely pleasant place to walk; the grass and trees soften the harshness of the ancient stones, and offer a restful change from the bright sunlight. The city's tremendous history is ever-present—but in the Forum it can be contemplated with a degree of serenity.

Temple of Antoninus and Faustina (above) and Titus' arch (centre) in the Forum Romanum. Below: old representation of the Colosseum. Far right: exterior and interior views of the Colosseum.

God's largest church
ST PETER'S IN ROME

It is said on the Tiber that Rome really had three founders. As well as Romulus and Remus, the legendary twins who marked the beginning of ancient Rome's development into the capital of the world, the apostle Peter must also be included among its founders, for it was because of him that the city was later reborn after the fall of the Roman Empire and became important as the most magnificent city in Christendom. In honour of the third founder the largest and finest church in the world was built in Rome above his supposed grave during the sixteenth century. The best architects and most famous artists in Italy worked over a period of 120 years to complete St Peter's Church, San Pietro in Vaticano, at whose high altar the Pope, as head of the Roman Catholic Church, celebra[tes] mass and in which he announces dogmas and proclaims canoni[za]tions.

'In the Christian world there is no older or richer House of G[od] associated with greater events of world history.' Before the c[on]struction of the present church of St Peter a five-aisled basi[lica] also dedicated to St Peter, had been built in the same place, [near] the Circus of Nero, by Constantine the Great at the request of P[ope] Sylvester I. Countless emperors were crowned before the h[igh] altar of this church, including Charlemagne on whom Pope Le[o] placed the crown of Holy Roman Emperor on Christmas Day 8[00].

e Nicolas V wanted to replace the old church by a new and
er building. In 1452 work began on the plans of Bernardo
sellino but three years later, on the death of the Pope, they were
away with the walls standing hardly three feet above ground
l.

 was not until fifty years later that the building site came to life
n. Pope Julius II had decided to have an enormous monument
nimself built while he was still alive by the young sculptor
helangelo, whose statue of David set up in front of the Palazzo
chio in Florence had caused such a sensation. Michelangelo
 ordered to look for a suitable site and he suggested building

the burial chapel on the walls of the church. This reminded the
Pope of the old plans and he decided to have the work resumed.
A part of the new church of St Peter was to be reserved for the
proposed tomb. From the many designs for the church Julius II
selected Bramante's plans and on 18 April 1506 work began.

Bramante had suggested a church in the form of a Greek cross
with equal arms and an enormous main dome above the intersection;

**Above: St Peter's and St Peter's Square with the obelisk and Bernini's
colonnades.**

53

smaller domes were planned for the arms of the cross. However, Bramante died in 1514 and under his successors Raphael, Fra Gioconda da Verona and Giuliano da Sangallo, the ingenious plan was modified. For a long time there was controversy over whether or not a ground plan in the shape of a Latin cross was preferable. Michelangelo, who had been commissioned by Pope Paul III to supervise the construction, reverted to the Greek cross. The brilliant architect's most important contribution to St Peter's was the illustrious and, in spite of its size, apparently weightless dome above the papal altar which was finished by Michelangelo's successors.

In 1606 Pope Paul V ordered a return to the shape of the Latin cross. Then Carlo Maderna built the nave of the cathedral and the Baroque façade, which from close to at least, obscures the view of Michelangelo's dome. It was not until the church had already been consecrated on 18 November 1626 that Bernini, as Maderna's successor, was engaged to complete the building and its surroundings. He contributed the 95-foot-high tabernacle over the papal altar. Above all, however, he was responsible for the present appearance of St Peter's Square, the Piazza di San Pietro. He designed the splendid colonnades which frame the square with its unique impression of spaciousness. The designs for the 162 statues of saints on the balustrade were also his. The 269-foot-high obelisk in the centre of the square is Egyptian in origin. It was used by Caligula to grace Nero's Circus, and in 1586 was transported to its present site.

The cost of building the largest Christian church was about £25,000,000, raised to a large extent from the sale of indulgences. An inscription on the floor of the nave records the total length of the building as 636 feet. The church covers an area of 18,131 square yards, and the dome to the tip of the cross is 436 feet high.

In his work on church architecture which appeared a hundred years ago, Carl von Lützow wrote: 'A building, which, like St Peter's, owes its reputation primarily to its colossal size and the brilliance of its furnishings and decorations is more difficult than any other to describe in words—all the more so, as the basic shape in which it is laid out and the style in which it is thought out are, by their very nature, completely devoid of all individual characteristics and strive after universality.' Like successive critics of the building, Lützow lamented the fact that Bramante's ground plan in the shape of a Greek cross had been obliterated by the addition of the nave. 'One distinctly senses that the originally fundamental unifying idea was sacrificed to the absolute demand for a display of size and splendour.' On the other hand Jacob Burckhardt is of the opinion that the church's impression of spaciousness depends entirely on the lighting and the number of people. 'On Easter Sunday everybody knows that he is in the largest interior in the world.'

The general impression of the church, with its balanced proportions, its effects of perspective, of colour and of streaming light, on the impartial observer is spell-binding, and anyone who turns his attention to the individual parts of the building, the monuments and works of art, will experience this impression even more intensely. St Peter's, however, is not only a House of God and a masterpiece of architecture, but, above all, a symbol of the church's universality.

Above: Papal altar with Bernini's tabernacle. Below: view into the dome of St Peter's. Created by Michelangelo, it measures 137 feet in diameter. Far left, above: Tiber with Ponte Sant' Angelo and view of St Peter's. In the lower pictures are (left) ground plan and cross-section of the church and (right) a view of the oval of St Peter's Square and Rome's sea of houses from the dome of the cathedral.

Is Naples a beautiful city? If the question is taken too literally the answer has to be negative. On close scrutiny neither the old nor the new parts of Naples are strikingly beautiful—on the contrary, if one wanders down one of the miserable narrow little back streets it is impossible to understand the meaning of the melancholy saying, 'See Naples and die.' Even Karl Baedecker who, in his quest for noteworthy sights, combed through the 'New Town'—that is the meaning of its name—which dates back to a Greek settlement, reluctantly confirmed that the city had little charm. He found not a single building worthy of a two-star rating and only in his description of the art treasures of the famous Museo Nationale was the experienced guide generous in his praise. How is it then that Naples more than almost any other town has been praised by poets and painters in rapturous words and glowin[g] colours? 'Location and surroundings belong to the most beautifu[l] on earth,' Baedeker succinctly observed. Only by its situation o[n] the sweeping bay, with Vesuvius in the background, is Naple[s] transformed into a place of beauty, into the 'most serene town i[n] the world' (Melville). In 1787 Goethe wrote: 'The inhabitants o[f] Naples cannot be blamed for not wanting to move out of their tow[n] nor its poets for singing exaggerated praises of their home, n[or] could they be blamed even if there were a few more Vesuviuses i[n] the neighbourhood.

Vesuvius, that fateful mountain above Naples and potenti[al] threat to the whole bay—Goethe experienced it wild and furiou[s] 'We stood at a window of the upper floor with Vesuvius directly i[n]

Fateful mountain over Naples
VESUVIUS

ont of us. The flames of the descending lava glowed clearly in the
arkness and began to gild the accompanying smoke. The mountain
ged violently and above it hung an enormous, motionless cloud
steam, every line picked out and lit up as if by lightning by each
uption. From there to the sea ran a ribbon of fire and glowing
sts.'

The fire-spitting mountain produced its last significant eruption
1944. Since then it has behaved peaceably and not even the
ditional cloud of steam stands above the 4,156 foot high volcano
d its neighbouring peak, the 3,675 foot high Monte Somma, but
e inhabitants of the bay, whose safety is watched over by a
suvius observatory, know that this calm can be deceptive. Once
fore, during the years after the birth of Christ, it was assumed

that the volcano was extinct. At that time Strabo recorded that
there were soot-coloured stones to be seen and so there must once
have been craters of fire, but that the volcano had not been active
for a long time because it had exhausted its fuel.

There were many earthquakes, but no one ever associated them
with Vesuvius. On 24 August AD 79 the catastrophe happened:
in the early morning, when it was pouring with rain, Vesuvius
erupted. Vast quantities of ash merged with the rain-water forming

**The view of the bay is dominated by Vesuvius (right) and Monte
Somma. Since 1944 the crater above the 'most serene town in the
world' has been still.**

a river of mud which engulfed the spa town of Herculaneum; houses disappeared under a layer up to 65 feet deep. The town of Pompeii—its inhabitants numbered between 20,000 and 30,000—like the neighbouring town of Stabiae, was covered by piles of pumice and ashes. Rescue operations were useless because anyone who had remained in the three towns had perished. The number of dead has been estimated at 2,000. For a time attempts were made to save building materials, household goods and valuables from the area of Pompeii which had been buried only to the edge of the roofs. Then gradually Pompeii, Herculaneum and Stabiae were forgotten and it was not until 1,700 years after the catastrophe that they aroused any further interest—at first in amateur archaeologists, who had shafts driven into the ground here and there to search for antiquities, and later in scholars. To begin with only isolated points were tackled and it was only after 1860 that it was excavated systematically when Guiseppe Fiorelli was put in charge of the operation.

Ever since then the excavations have continued. Countless testimonies to human tragedies at the time of the catastrophe were found: the remains of people smothered in flight, children

surprised by death, slaves still in their chains, participants in a feast, and prisoners who had tried with their last strength to get free. Little by little the town was excavated. Houses and temples, taverns, libraries, palaces and theatres came almost undamaged to the light of day, revealing detailed evidence of how the inhabitants lived, ate, drank, worked, traded and loved at the time when Christ was alive. 'There have been many disasters in the world but few can have given so much pleasure to posterity,' Goethe remarked after his second visit to Pompeii.

Left, top to bottom: street with stepping stones in Pompeii; interior of a typical house; wall mosaic from Herculaneum; aerial view of Pompeii. Above: Apollo's temple and statue in Pompeii. Left-hand page, above: view of the Vesuvius crater. Below: photograph of the last serious eruption of Vesuvius in 1872.

Pinnacle of European civilization
THE ACROPOLIS

Anyone who mentions Ancient Greece thinks first and foremost of Athens and anyone who thinks of Athens thinks of the Acropolis with its famous temples—the epitome of classical symmetry and elegant beauty, the 'tangible pinnacle of European civilization', the 'symbol of true humanity', the centre of the classical world. According to the myth, Athena and Poseidon once contended for possession of Athens. To demonstrate his power Poseidon touched the rock of the Acropolis with his trident, immediately causing a spring to appear on the spot he had touched. Athena, on the other hand, planted an olive tree in the barren rock. It instantly began to sprout luxuriantly, and Poseidon admitted

defeat. The holy olive tree of Athena survived all the plots aga the Acropolis. Even when the Persians burnt it after they had ta Athens it had already produced a new shoot a yard long by the r day—a miracle which is supposed to have spurred on the people Athens to renew their resistance.

Excavations have shown that the yellowish blue limestone c of the Acropolis (the name means 'upper city' and was used many citadels in ancient Greece), rising 511 feet above sea le and 262 feet above Athens, must have been inhabited as far b as the Neolithic period, some 4,000 years ago. The first forti palace was built during the Mycenaean period and there are

ains of walls from this time (about 1,200 BC). Amongst other
gs the Greeks of the sixth century BC built a temple to Athena,
onumental gateway and a shrine to Nike, but none of these
dings was to stand for long. In 480–479 they were razed to the
und by the Persians. Themistocles and Cimon had only the outer
s rebuilt and the site of the buildings levelled off, using the
ains of the old temples as building material. Later excavations
he 'Persian rubble' produced valuable clues to the appearance
he initial layout of the Greek Acropolis. Among other things, it
discovered from these excavations that the sculptures on the
nal temples had been painted in bright colours.

Pericles, from 461 BC the military commander and dictatorial
ruler of Athens, constructed on the mountain stronghold of the
Acropolis those buildings of Greece's classical era whose impressive
remains can still be admired today. In 448 he founded a building
consortium, to which prominent architects, sculptors (including
Phidias) and painters belonged.

The Parthenon, the high temple of Athena, was built first. Ictinus

**The temple area of the Acropolis above Athens: in the centre the
Parthenon.**

drew up the plans and Callicrates supervised the actual building operations, while the sculptures were designed by Phidias and made in his workshop. On an enormous three-level substructure with an area 230 feet by 100 feet stood forty-six Doric columns over 30 feet high. The sculptures in the tympanums and friezes belong to the greatest sculptural achievements in the world. Above the deep red walls of the interior there was a painted, wooden, coffered ceiling. The focal point of the temple was the 42-foot-high statue of Athena Parthenos by Phidias, which was made of gold and ivory. The 7·5-mm-thick gold plates could be removed to check the weight. This actually happened in the year 433 when Phidias was accused of having taken some of the gold.

During the fifth century the Parthenon was converted into a Christian church, and the Turks made it into a mosque in 1456,

As the second building of the Pericles era the temple of Ath Nike was commissioned. The architect of this small Ionic build was again Callicrates. On an area measuring 16 feet by 26 feet built an elegant temple with 13-foot-high columns and a 17-in high frieze. During the Turkish occupation the temple of Nike v torn down and the blocks of stone were used to build a basti In 1835–6 the German archaeologist Ross dismantled it a reconstructed the temple.

Work on the temple of Nike was protracted over sixteen ye because halfway through the construction it was decided to co plete the extensive propylaeum first. This task was alloted Mnesicles who designed an enormous propylaeum with twe Doric columns on the façade. On each side of the entrance th were to have been rectangular, pillared halls but they were ne

building a slender minaret next to it. When they were besieged by the Venetians under Count Königsmarck they put all their stocks of gunpowder and all their important people into the Parthenon mosque, hoping that the besiegers would not dare seize the temple. However, it never came to that, for according to an old chronicle, 'A lieutenant from Lüneburg grew impatient to throw bombs into the temple. The explosion of the gunpowder almost completely destroyed the Parthenon. All the restoration of later years—the most important move to save the Parthenon was instigated by Leo von Klenze in 1834 on the instructions of Ludwig I of Bavaria—could only compensate to a limited extent for the destruction of 1687.

finished. In the left wing of the propylaeum the Pinacotheca, first art gallery in the world, was set up.

As the fourth principal building of the temple area the Erechth was planned, a temple consecrated to the worship of Posei Erechtheus and Athena Polias. In this case the building operati were supervised by Mnesicles, but work had hardly started when Peloponnesian War, a war between Athens and Sparta which las almost thirty years, broke out and building was brought to a In 429 Pericles died of the plague. It was not until 404 that pe came—and for Athens, humiliation. The economic strength of metropolis was exhausted. However, the Athenians used a l

use after their victory over the Spartan
...t to complete, within the space of two
...rs, the Erechtheum. Philocles com-
...ted the work started by Mnesicles, a
...lding with an irregular ground plan
...corated with Ionic columns. The peculiar
...pe of the temple was a result of the
...d to house several shrines, including
...spring of Poseidon, the olive tree of
...hena and the grave of King Cecrops.

...nstruction of the Acropolis by
...rsch (right). The centre row of
...tographs shows the three most im-
...ant temples: (left to right) the
...htheum, temple of Nike and the
...henon. Above right: a capital from
...lumn; fragment of sculpture from
...cropolis, now in the Agora Museum.

Roadway through the Alps
THE MONT BLANC TUNNEL

For a fifth of the 580,000,000 inhabitants of Europe 16 July 1965 was a day of celebration: a hundred million French, Italians and Swiss were filled with enthusiasm by the opening of the Mont Blanc Tunnel. Great convoys of cars decorated with little flags travelled for the first time along the two 13-foot-wide asphalt carriageways under the highest mountain in Europe (15,771 feet).

The 6½-mile-long Mont Blanc Tunnel links France with Italy—more precisely, Chamonix in Savoy with Courmayeur in the Aosta Valley. The travelling time between Rome and Paris, the capitals of the two countries responsible for building it, has been reduced by twenty hours. The new Alpine tunnel is one of the most recent assaults on the greatest traffic obstacle in Europe, the 375-mile-long and 5,000 to 15,750 foot high Alpine chain. Tunnels through the Alpine massif have always been a delicate question in the field of high politics, and some governments in the past have burned their fingers. To countries which built them they brought tremendous economic advantages. At the same time, however, each new tunnel through the Alps also threatened the European balance of trade, often causing pointless but nonetheless real 'tunnel feuds' between the countries concerned.

France gave the lead with the Mont Cenis Tunnel which was completed in 1871. For a decade it enabled the French to dominate trade between England and Western Europe on the one side, and the Mediterranean and the East on the other. From 1878 onwards the Swiss entered into competition with the St Gotthard Tunnel which brought advantages above all to the German Empire. Later, much to the annoyance of the Germans, the Swiss and Italians together built the longest tunnel in the world, the 62,335-foot-long Simplon railway tunnel. Nowadays, however, with the enormous increase in car ownership interest is in road rather than railway tunnels.

French and Italian engineers had been preoccupied by the Mont Blanc Tunnel project for a long time when in March 1953 the method of construction and division of costs were agreed in Paris. The city of Geneva, because it also had a keen interest in the building of the tunnel, provided a part of the costs, which were estimated at a total of £35,000,000.

The French and Italian drilling gangs were to meet 18,380 feet inside the mountain. For the Italians Mont Blanc was a particularly tough assignment: they first had to work their way through hard schist formations. Over a period of six years mobile scaffolds, on which up to twenty automatic high performance drills were mounted, slowly ate their way further and further into the mountain. Special machines cleared a total of over 35,000,000 cubic feet of rubble out of the tunnel. As in every major tunnel-building operation, there were numerous incidents. Floods and landslides almost buried the intrepid human moles, and the Italian work camp was on one occasion demolished by avalanches.

Nevertheless, the enormous expenditure and immense costs have been amply rewarded and the Mont Blanc Tunnel has not proved to be a bad risk for those who had it built. Of the fourteen passes through the Alps only five stay open throughout the year. For anyone wanting to travel quickly and comfortably from north to south, the route through Mont Blanc is ideal; but of course comfort and speed have to be paid for. Nobody could quarrel with that—but there have been complaints from some quarters that the high tolls levied on private and commercial vehicles travelling through Mont Blanc (between £3 and £15) have long since repaid the major part of the original cost.

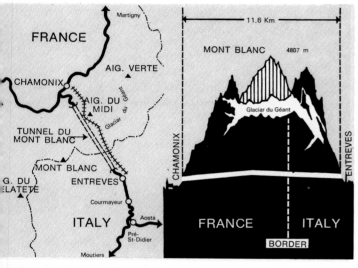

Top to bottom: pipes bring in air; plans for the tunnel; welding; opening procession of 16 July 1965. Far left: tunnel mouth during building operations; drills mounted on scaffolds eat their way through the rock (below).

Pages 64-5: entrance to Mont Blanc Tunnel on the French side; above it the 'Aiguille du Midi' in the Mont Blanc massif.

The 'Lady of Paris', as the French are in the habit of calling the slender tower, designed by the engineer Eiffel, was inaugurated in 1899 at the World Exhibition in Paris, and so is now quite an old lady. In spite of this the Eiffel Tower has lost nothing of its unique charm, technical significance, or of its symbolic power. On the contrary, never since the completion of the tower have such throngs of visitors—over two million a year—been hauled up to the spacious platforms of the steel scaffold in the squeaking lurching lifts as today. Paris without the Eiffel Tower would be inconceivable.

The first concrete proposal to build a tower of a thousand feet was put forward in 1833 by an Englishman called Trevithick, this scheme came no nearer to realization despite the notion building a thousand foot tower for the world exhibition of 187? Philadelphia. In 1884 the first draft for a 984-foot-high iron to was worked out in Eiffel's engineering office. There were m other schemes. The people, for example, were very keen on idea of a 'sun tower', 984 feet high, with an enormous beacor the top which would transform Paris night into bright dayligh was suggested that one of the floors of this tower should be set as a hospital for high altitude treatment, but the minister of tr who was responsible for the exhibition, favoured Eiffel's plar

THE EIFFEL TOWER

s decided to build the tower on a square with sides measuring
) feet. A hundred and seven possible sites were thoroughly
mined. The exhibition committee wanted to have a tower
dging the Seine, but this plan had to be abandoned because of
poor condition of the land on the banks of the Seine. Eventually
Field of Mars, which in any case had been planned as the
ibition site, was selected.

t was not by chance that the 54-year-old engineer and designer
xandre Gustave Eiffel was chosen to build the symbol for the
ibition. Long before this tower was built he was considered
world's leading authority on iron structures. He was celebrated

as the 'Engineer of the Universe' and made his name as a founder
of aerodynamics. Dozens of steel constructions throughout the
world were the work of Eiffel's firm, but in spite of this, it was as
the architect of the building named after him that Eiffel was to be
known best. 'This tower is still killing me,' he moaned. 'As if I had
never achieved anything else.'

Alexandre Gustave Eiffel was born in Dijon in 1832. His French
biographers discovered that he was descended from a German
called Hans Heinrich Bönickhausen who as a young man during the
reign of Louis XIV left his home town of Marmagen in the Eifel
district and emigrated to France. In memory of his Rhineland home

the immigrant enlarged his name to Eifel-Bönickhausen and until 1880 the family retained this double-barrelled name. Then Alexandre Gustave Eiffel dropped the original family name and simply called himself Eiffel.

In 1886 preparations for the tower were begun. Stone foundations measuring 280 square feet had to be constructed to support the four piers. On the Seine side of the Field of Mars they were sunk 45 feet into the ground and on the other side 30 feet. By 30 June 1887, two years before the opening of the exhibition, the work on the foundations was complete.

Public reaction to the tower was varied. While the project was officially heralded with premature praise as a 'Triumph of industrial civilization', a 'masterpiece of the new iron architecture' and a 'symbol of the reawakened France' (after the defeat of 1871), distinguished writers, painters, sculptors and architects found themselves united in a protest movement even before the first sod had been turned. In a sensational interview Guy de Maupassant, one of the signatories of the protest, made fun of the 'frightful and feeble pyramid'. Eiffel and the directors of the exhibition had great difficulty in defending the tower which their opponents called a 'building of stupefying absurdity' that 'dominates Paris like a gigantic black chimney.

But the protests achieved nothing, for backing the Société

tons—an immense mass of iron, yet a construction light as filigree The air in a 984 foot high cylinder with a circumference describin the rectangle of piers would be significantly heavier than the whol Eiffel Tower.

In order to finish the tower on time it was necessary, even durin the severe winter of 1888–9, to work ten hours a day. On 31 Marc Gustave Eiffel was able to hoist the tricolour to the top of th tower and everything was ready for the opening of the exhibitio on 6 May 1889. Not only the influx of visitors (in the first year th Eiffel Tower Company had already recouped more than its capit outlay), but also the sale of small models of the Tower became thriving industry.

The Eiffel Tower has become an integral part of Paris, thoug there are still occasional protests that it disfigures the appearanc of the city. There is a well-known anecdote about the man wh cannot bear the Eiffel Tower but is forced to climb it every da because it is the only place in Paris which does not have a view the tower. The 'Lady of Paris' has been the subject of art and literatur The talk is no longer of 'stupefying absurdity', but rather reflects sort of loyalty to this great witness of the iron age which has becom even more a part of Paris now that, in the era of atomic physics ar worldwide travel, it has long since ceased to represent a sensation technological innovation.

de la Tour Eiffel, founded with a capital of 5,100,000 francs, was the French government. The scheme went ahead as planned and one year after work on the iron structure had started, the first platform was joined to the four enormous supporting piles, Gustave Eiffel let off a celebratory rocket. To this first storey, standing at a height of 190 feet, were added the second (380 feet) and third (895 feet) platforms of the tower.

For two years forty draughtsmen worked on the drawings for the 15,000 components. A factory in Clichy produced the finished parts which fitted exactly and only needed to be screwed or riveted together on the building site. The finished tower weighed over 9,600

Fireworks were let off and the Eiffel Tower was floodlit for opening in 1889 (above left) at the world exhibition in Paris. Abo latticed construction of the tower - the first example of a p fabricated steel-skeleton building, prototype for many skyscrape Far right: the Eiffel Tower as seen by visitors to Paris. Right, top bottom: work on the final stages of the tower; Gustave Ei hoisting a flag to the top for the first time; bust of Eiffel.

Pages 68-69: Paris at sunset, with the floodlit Eiffel Tower.

Focal point of Paris

ARC DE TRIOMPHE

When Napoleon I commissioned a building he was one of the most tyrannical taskmasters the world has ever known. His blunt instructions to Chalgrin, the architect who was to build for him 'the biggest arch of all countries and all times' in the centre of Paris, were that 'It should be built in honour of *me*, not in honour of the architect!' In building the Arc de Triomphe it was the great Corsican general's wish to establish a colossal monument to his victories and battles. There had already been one such monument—the small triumphal arch which stood in front of the Louvre in the Place de Carrousel—but Napoleon found that his glory had long outgrown this.

Chalgrin's design was inspired by contemporary taste and the emperor's own predilection for ancient Rome. He created an almost embarrassingly exact copy of the arches found in Classical Ro[me] only much, much bigger. Work on its construction was started [in] 1811, the tragic year when the Grande Armée set off for Russ[ia] but Napoleon was never to see the completion of his triump[hal] arch. His fortunes declined and his ambitious plans for an extens[ive] palace behind the Arc de Triomphe, which was to be more splen[did] than Versailles and more impressive than the Louvre, collected d[ust] in the state archives.

It was not until twenty-five years later that the citizen ki[ng,] Louis Philippe, had work resumed on the largest triumphal arch [in] the world. His stonemasons put the finishing touches to the colos[sal] reliefs on the pillars, sides and cornice, which depict Napoleo[n's] coronation, battles which took place when France was a repu[blic]

when it was an empire and, time after time, the glorious de-
~ure and happy return of the army. The names of 172 battles and
~ generals immortalized in the stone of the arch emphasize the
entirely peaceful nature of the Arc de Triomphe.
~day the silver-grey colossus, which stands 160 feet high, 147
~ wide and 72 feet deep, is regarded as a masterpiece of neo-
~sical architecture. Cold and majestic it looms in the Paris sky.
~ands in the centre of the Place de l'Etoile at the intersection of
~e large avenues laid out in the shape of a star. Day and night
~nstant flashing stream of cars pours from the Etoile into the
~nificent and perfectly straight Champs Elysées.
~rom time to time the gendarmes direct the never-ending stream
~affic to one side while a foreign state visitor lays a wreath on

the tomb of the Unknown Warrior under the vaulted arch. On 11
November 1920 the remains of an unidentified French soldier who
was killed at Verdun were buried there. The bluish glow of an
eternal flame flickers in front of the tomb, and it is respect for the
dead, not an emperor's intoxication with triumph, which makes
the Arc de Triomphe France's national monument.

The Avenue des Champs Elysées leads directly to the Arc de Triomphe (left). Among the most impressive sculptures on the Arc de Triomphe is the 'Marseillaise' (right) by Rudé.

À TOUTES LES GLOIRES DE LA FRANCE.

The most magnificent palace in the world

VERSAILLES

The region was marshy and unhealthy. For many miles around there was no running water, fever was rife and the scanty vegetation was hardly sufficient to support the animals which Louis XIII and his retinue hunted. The only building of any significance was a modest hunting lodge belonging to the king.

In this inhospitable clime Louis XIV built Versailles, the most magnificent palace in the world, a symbol of the age of absolutism, 'immense and at the same time harmonious'. The technical difficulties did not concern the 'Sun King' and in France his will was absolute. In his opinion all that was needed to create a grandiose palace on the waterless plateau was the right people and adequate funds.

In 1661 the architect Le Vau started with the building of the first phase in association with the painter Le Brun, who was responsible

6,000 horses were used to pull carts containing stones, beams a[n]d marble blocks; and the building costs amounted to over £60,000,0[00]. Little by little a palace, unlike anything belonging to any other rul[er] arose. It had a 635-foot-long main front punctuated by 375 window[s,] enormous courtyards, numerous annexes and wings, and an aven[ue] which led straight as a Roman road to Paris.

The architect Jules Hardouin-Mansart, Le Vau's success[or] completed construction of the palace. Painters and sculpto[rs,] marble-cutters and goldsmiths, engravers and plasterers create[d a] scene of unparalleled perfection. White and gold were the p[re]dominant colours. Not only walls and ceilings gleamed in wh[ite] and gold; the king even had the water deities seated above t[he] marble pools in the garden gilded, and golden decorations crown[ed]

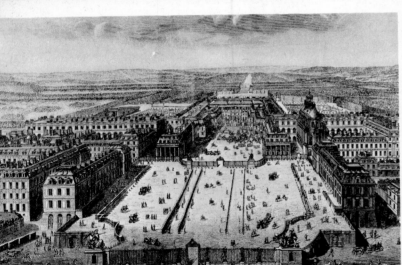

for the furnishings and decorations, and the landscape gardener Le Nôtre, who was responsible for designing the gardens and fountains in the enormous grounds. Almost every day the king, a conscientious if tiresome employer, appeared on the building site to find out how the work was progressing. Nothing could discourage him—not the immense cost which forced him to have his silver tableware melted down for coins; not the fever epidemic which struck the throng of workers; not even the mass desertion of craftsmen during the severe winters of 1678 and 1684.

Some 3,600 people, recruited from every part of France, were employed on the building which was to glorify the Sun King;

the dormer windows in the roof.

The construction of the fountains demanded an unpreceden[ted] technological effort. As there was no running water in the immed[iate] vicinity of the palace, it had to be brought from the Seine. A pump[ing] station was built near Marly and its 221 pumps were used to r[aise] water from the Seine over the 177 foot high banks. From he[re it] flowed to Versailles at a rate of 80,000 cubic yards a day. [The] 'Machine of Marly' invented by René Rennequin, an enginee[r of] Arab descent, functioned perfectly until the year 1804, when it [was] rebuilt, and after that lasted a further fifty years or so without ser[ious] defect. It also outlived the abortive attempt to pipe water to Versa[illes]

On 6 May 1682 Louis XIV moved his court to Versailles 'for ever'—
t brilliant court without which it is impossible to imagine the
n of the Sun King, just as the court without Versailles is un-
nkable. Kinsmen of the most distinguished aristocratic families
d for the honour of serving the king: 'The nobility submitted to
etiquette no less strict than that of the Spanish court and were
ud participants in a cult of the king. Getting up, meal times,
ng to bed became ceremonies which were carried out every day
ording to the same unalterable and minutely prescribed ritual.
courtier were to walk through Louis XIV's room and pass the
al bed, he would genuflect as if he were in front of the altar in
hurch.' (Georges Pages). Goethe called this pomp and cere-
nial, which today seem so incredibly strange, 'necessary factors

taken to the Tuileries. Within a short time the number of residents
at Versailles had fallen by half. During the war of 1870–1 the
palace was the seat of the German command and on 18 January
1871 the restoration of the German Empire was proclaimed in the
Mirror Room. In the same magnificent room the 'Treaty of Versailles'
between Germany and the victorious allies was signed on 28 June
1919 at the end of the First World War.

Versailles, now an important tourist attraction and museum, was
in its time copied all over Europe. Whether Schönbrunn Palace in
Vienna, the King's Castle in Madrid, Caserta near Naples, Sans-
Souci in Potsdam—everywhere the same extensive palaces in the
style of Hardouin-Mansart and the same magnificent grounds like
those Le Nôtre laid out for Louis XIV are to be found.

certain stage in civilization'. None of them, apparently, perceived
this 'civilization' was racing to the edge of the abyss. In just
a century Louis XIV's 'for ever' had come to an end.
agnificent festivities took place in the countless rooms and
mous grounds of the palace. However, Versailles with the small
hbouring palace of Trianon was not only the centre for the
vities of a lively retinue; from here—at a calculated distance
the people and the capital, Paris—France was ruled and the
commanded in many wars. The significance of Versailles
inued until, on 6 October 1789, after the outbreak of the
ch Revolution, Louis XVI was dragged from his palace and

**Sea and river gods populate the pools before the Garden Front of
the palace. Pictured above is the representation of the Seine in
front of the garden portal. Far left: view of the palace from the
Parterre de Latonne (above); view of the palace in 1715 (etching by
P. Menant). Left: chandelier in front of the entrance to the Mirror
Room.**

**Pages 76-77: view of the Courtyard of Honours and main entrance to
Palace of Versailles: in the centre a statue of Louis XIV on horse-
back.**

Electricity from the sea
LA RANCE TIDAL POWER STATION

It has long been one of man's dreams to utilize the tidal energy which Nature supplies free of charge. Five hundred years ago there were already machines operated by sea power which made use of the difference in water level produced by the ebb and flow of the tide. One of them, the watermill at Saint Suliac, which was operated by the flood tide, can still be seen today. It stands in the mouth of the River Rance and the engineers at the world's first large-scale tidal power station proudly direct the visitor's attention to this adjacent precursor.

It was quite by chance that Robert Gibrat, a thirty-six-year-old engineer who in 1940 had been put in charge of the department for power in the French ministry of public works, stumbled on the long-forgotten plans for a tidal power station. Gibrat designed a type of dam suitable for blocking off a bay or arm of the sea. The volumes of water flowing in with the incoming tide and out again with the outgoing tide were to be converted into electricity by turbines.

After a great deal of research the young engineer chose the River Rance as the site: the conditions here were ideal. About six miles above its mouth in the English Channel the Rance broadens out into a basin over 3,000 feet wide which could be made into a reservoir if it were blocked off by a dam immediately above St Malo. The difference in level between high and low tide was 42 feet—greater than anywhere else in the world. Under favourable conditions about 235,000 cubic yards of water per second flowed into the Rance when the tide came in. Gibrat founded a private research committee to further his plans. It was later taken over by the French power concern Electricité de France.

The author, Jules Verne, who came from St Malo and wrote countless novels set in a technological Utopia, would have been delighted by the experiments which were to follow. In a deserted harbour bay in St Servan a scale model of the proposed power station was built. From this it was concluded that building a power station on a river bed which was constantly submerged would not be entirely without its problems.

In 1961 work began in the mouth of the Rance. On the basis of the results of the experiment it had been decided to build two bow-shaped catch dams in the middle of the river bed, which at this point is over 2,000 yards wide. Reinforced concrete cylinders 65 to 80 feet high and 30 feet in diameter were so arranged in the river bed that they stood 45 feet above the average water level. The hollow centres were filled with thousands of tons of sand. As a result of the excavations an elliptical basin was left which could be pumped dry when the two dams had been caulked. In this basin the power station was built. It is in the form of a concave concrete dam and contains the twenty-four turbines. The turbines operate both when the reservoir fills up as the tide comes in and when it empties as the tide goes out. Water can also be pumped in to the basin from the sea if the natural input is low.

The turbines produce about 540,000,000 kilowatt hours a year. The first tidal power station in the world functions as smoothly as if such techniques were as old as the sea.

The famous monastery-fortress Mont St Michel (above) was spoken of when a site for the power station was being selected. Bow-shaped dams (centre) enabled the building site for the power station dam to be drained. Below: the control room of the power station regulates the ebb and flow of water. Right-hand page: view over the hollow dam (above), in which the twenty-four turbines were built (below right). Left: watermill of St Suliac.

Pages 80–81: on the in-coming tide sea water flows into the basin.

Le Corbusier's pilgrims' chapel
RONCHAMP

In 1950 Swiss-French architect Le Corbusier (his real name was Charles Edouard Jeanneret) had only designed secular buildings and come to terms with the building problems posed by cities. Works like the Swiss House at the Cité Universitaire in Paris or the Unité d'Habitation in Marseilles had made him world famous. He was, therefore, rather hesitant when he was asked to build a new chapel to replace the church of Nôtre Dame du Haut in Ronchamp, not far from Belfort, a place of pilgrimage which had been destroyed during the Second World War.

Once he had seen the place his mind was made up, and in June 1950 he produced the first sketches. They departed so completely from the conventional and traditional that Le Corbusier himself spoke of a building designed 'with rashness, certainly, but with courage'. The interior of the church creates the impression of a 'cave without a mountain', and the shape of the exterior is more reminiscent of a modern sculpture than a church. But the Archbishop of Besançon and the building committee of his diocese approved the daring plans, and after a construction period of four years the building was consecrated. Its dimensions are relatively modest, the 80-foot by 50 foot nave holding at most 250 people. For the great flocks of pilgrims an altar and chancel were built in the open air.

'Not for one moment did I think of creating anything that would cause a sensation,' Le Corbusier professed, but for all that during the years following the completion of the chapel there was hardly a building in the world which was more harshly criticized or more highly praised than Nôtre Dame du Haut of Ronchamp. The complete asymmetry of the building, the rejection of the conventional bell tower (the three towers serve only as light shafts for the altars), the roof which appears to be upside down because it rises at the edges and dips in the middle, the almost bare interior—everything that horrified the critics reminded them of Picasso.

Le Corbusier did not deny certain connections: 'Abstract art, which nowadays quite rightly arouses heated discussion, is the reason why Ronchamp exists.' He had explained on a previous occasion 'One does not bring about a revolution by flying into a rage, one brings about a revolution by finding the solution.'

He had the good fortune to find his strongest supporters amongst his employers. 'At first one is surprised by the extreme novelty of these shapes,' wrote the French Dominican, M. A. Couturier. 'However, one very soon realizes that here the surfaces and shapes evolve with the sensitivity and freedom of living organisms, while at the same time remaining subdued by the discipline which controls the function and purpose of the structure. The religious nature is revealed in every part, not least in the novelty, the unfamiliarity of the form.

To anyone who expects a chapel of pilgrimage to be splendid and magnificent, Ronchamp will be a disappointment. The building high above the woods of Cherimont is not revealed at a glance. Above all, the chapel is a functional building, designed to fulfil its duties in the best possible way, but it is also more than that: 'A vessel of tranquility, of grace. A longing to reach through the language of architecture the feelings aroused by this place.' (Le Corbusier).

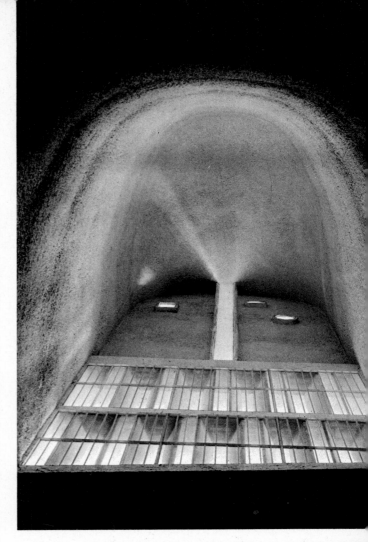

The church towers, below which the altars stand, act as light shafts (above). Below: view of the outside with the overhanging roof. Right-hand page: light and shade produce the chapel's singular impression of space (above). Below left: one of the colourful portals. The altars were placed below the three towers of the chapel of pilgrimage (below right).

As enigmatic as they are enormous, they tower above the rolling plain in the county of Wiltshire in southern England, thirty enormous blocks standing on end, each over 12 feet high and up to 9 feet wide.

What purpose did these giant stones serve in the dim past? Were they a temple and sacrificial altar? Were they the scene of the death rites of the Bronze Age people? Or were they nothing less than a sophisticated prehistoric observatory? No one can say. But on one thing the experts are agreed: Stonehenge is the most beautiful and most impressive relic of megalithic civilization that can be seen in Europe. From 3000 BC this prehistoric civilization, which practised worship of the dead, erected its own eternal monuments in the form of enormous structures of megaliths (large stones) in France, Spain and northern Europe.

The carbon-dating method has shown when Stonehenge was probably built—about 1600 BC. Modern research methods have revealed that altogether thirty blocks of the outer circle and the forty-nine smaller ones of the inner ring were painstakingly hewn entirely with stone tools. But how the architects of Stonehenge devised a means of bringing the giant blocks of stone, each weighing several tons, from the quarries in the mountains of Prescelli Myndd in Wales, over a

hundred miles away, no one has yet established. Speculation has been unceasing and numerous theories have been advanced; but the stones seem likely to keep their secrets.

The giant stones of Stonehenge were erected over 3,500 years ago (right and above). To this day it is not known for certain what purpose they served.

Witness of the Stone Age culture

STONEHENGE

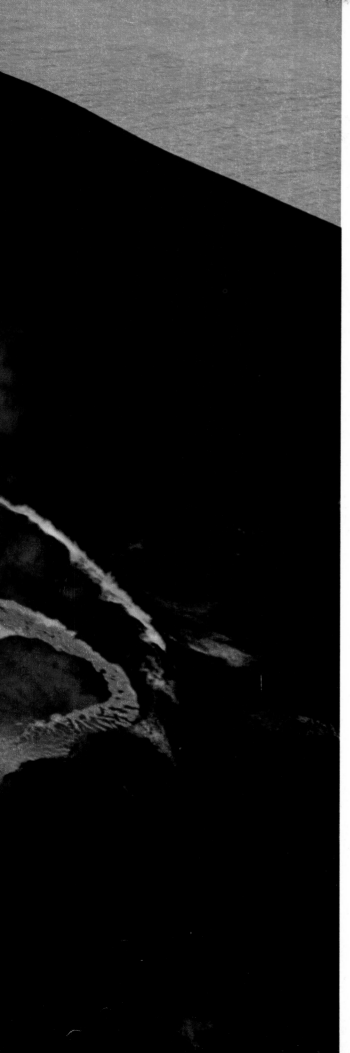

Birth of an island
SURTSEY

For the Icelanders a volcanic eruption is nothing out of the ordinary. On the 'island of fire', on the Arctic Circle, there are about 150 volcanoes which have been active at various times since the Ice Age and even in the time since the country was first colonized thirty volcanoes have made their presence felt with varying degrees of frequency. On average over the past centuries an eruption has occurred every five years.

In spite of being quite used to volcanic activity, the Icelanders themselves were surprised when they read in the newspapers about the latest volcanic eruption. Early in the morning of 14 November 1963 a fishing boat discovered an active volcano in the open North Atlantic, 25 miles south of Iceland. Geologists confirmed that the sea at this point was over 400 feet deep. On the first day only clouds of steam and smoke were visible. On the second day a whole island 1,640 feet long and 30 feet high emerged from the water. It grew rapidly and on the third day the cloud of smoke above the island (it must have been 30 feet high) could be seen from Reykjavik, 25 miles away. The new volcano was named Surtur after the principal fire giant of Germanic mythology and the island, logically enough, was called Surtsey, Surtur's Island.

In the first three months there were eruptions from three different craters. In April 1964 the volcano stopped spitting out ashes and pumice and, after a short interval, began to produce red and white hot basalt lava which ran down into the sea and made it boil, causing enormous clouds of steam to rise into the sky. Within the space of a year more than a thousand million cubic feet of lava were brought up. By April 1965 the area of the island was one square mile with a sheer 45-foot cliff in the south. The island's permanence finally seemed assured.

The first visitors to Surtsey were two reporters from a French magazine. During the interval between two eruptions they ventured across to the dangerous island and hoisted the tricolour. Seals were the first animals to make use of Surtsey's warm beach for a doze. Then numerous sea birds gradually settled in, but all the guests on Surtsey were forced to move out when, 800 yards to the east, a second island emerged from the Atlantic. Its volcano covered Surtsey with an eight-inch thick carpet of ash, but before the new little island could be given a name it sank back into the depths of the ocean. In its place a third island appeared at the end of December 1965, and six months later it had reached a size of 25 acres.

The mainland of Iceland, with an area of 39,809 square miles, also owes its existence to volcanic action. The oldest rocks on the island are barely more than 60,000,000 years old. Large areas of the country were formed during the last million years and a tenth of Iceland's surface is covered by lava streams which are less than 10,000 years old. Almost every kind of volcano is found in Iceland but the most common are the rift-volcanoes which can become active in up to a hundred individual vents in long rows of craters which throw out enormous masses of basalt lava. The last catastrophe occurred in 1783–4 when the crater of Laki erupted, covering a large area of land with streams of lava. Clouds of ashes were carried as far as Africa, 75 per cent of the livestock and 9,000 people died

An island is born. The crater of Surtur on 15 September 1964, ten months after the first eruption of the new volcano off the coast of Iceland.

during the famine which followed. Today there are no longer any active volcanoes in the basalt area, but the seething underworld is manifest in the hissing geysers and bubbling craters of mud. Many of the hot springs have been harnessed and used for heating in towns and villages. Lacking both railways and an army the country has few power problems. However, the fraught question remains: where will the next volcano erupt?

On the first day of eruptions (far left above), 14 November 1963, and on the third day (centre above) only steam and smoke can be distinguished from the air. The photograph of the aircraft circling the cloud (above) was also taken on the third day. Centre below: the crater of the Surtur on 25 April 1965. Far left below: Surtsey at the beginning of July 1965 with the lagoon and the second, significantly smaller island.

THINGVELLIR

The oldest parliament in the world, Iceland's Althing, held its first session in the year AD 930, about sixty years after the Norwegians had started to colonize the country. The assembly took place not in a permanent building but under the open sky at a spot which had been selected by Grim Geitskór, a farmer. The meeting place, about thirty miles from where Reykjavik now stands, was a three-mile-long ravine in a vast field of volcanic lava. Near this ravine, which was called Everyman Gorge because all the free men in the country could fit into it at the same time, the Icelandic meeting place, Thingvellir, was established.

Until the year 1798, when because of an earthquake the Althing moved to Reykjavik, the annual assembly took place at the Everyman Gorge. It was here that legal disputes were settled, the 'pro-

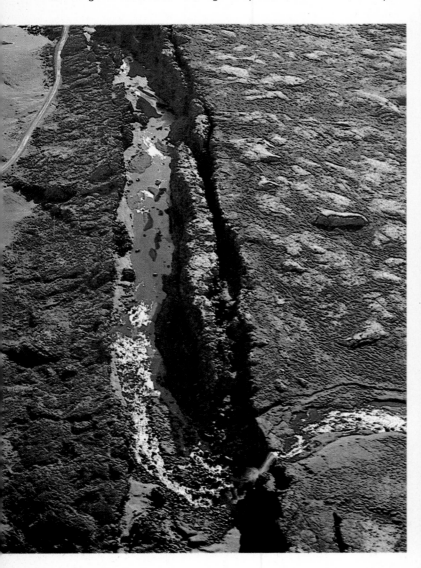

claimer of laws' quoting the laws from memory, and duels took place, but there were also performances by jugglers and recitations by bards of their latest epics. For centuries Thingvellir was the focal point of the 'country without a capital'

Today people from Reykjavik make their Sunday outings to the Everyman Gorge, not forgetting to visit the Öxará waterfall which was long ago created artificially by diverting the little Öxará River over the steep edge of the ravine.

The Everyman Gorge (right) with Thingvellir, the ancient Icelandic meeting place. Above: aerial photograph of the Öxará waterfall pouring into the gorge.

One third of the surface of Yugoslavia is covered with karst. The limestone area with its thousands of caves and rivers extends from Triglav to the Albanian mountains. Karst has been compared to an enormous petrified bath sponge. The 1,000 foot thick stratum contains a network of endless passages which absorb the surface water.

Whole rivers disappear below the surface of the earth, where they carve out passages, caves and gullies in the rock, plunge over cataracts and then pour into the sea. The caves of Postojna, formerly known as the Adelsberg Grottos, were carved by the River Pivka, a classic example of a river which has hollowed out the karst interior. The calcareous water dripping off the ceiling has created a veritable labyrinth of fantastic stalagmites and stalactites, columns and curtains, magnificent halls and chambers. About fourteen miles have been explored but the Postojna cave system, which was known as long ago as the Middle Ages and is one of the largest in the world, undoubtedly has further surprises in store. The most beautiful passages can be viewed from a small electric railway. The chambers have been dubbed with labels from the upper world, such as 'Cathedral', 'Paradise Grotto' and 'Ballroom'. In the 'Congress Room' the pot-

holers who explored the caves used to confer, and in the floodlit aquarium of the 'Great Hall' one can watch the grotto olm, a curious amphibious animal that has never seen the light of day.

Under floodlight the Caves of Postojna have a magical quality (right and above).

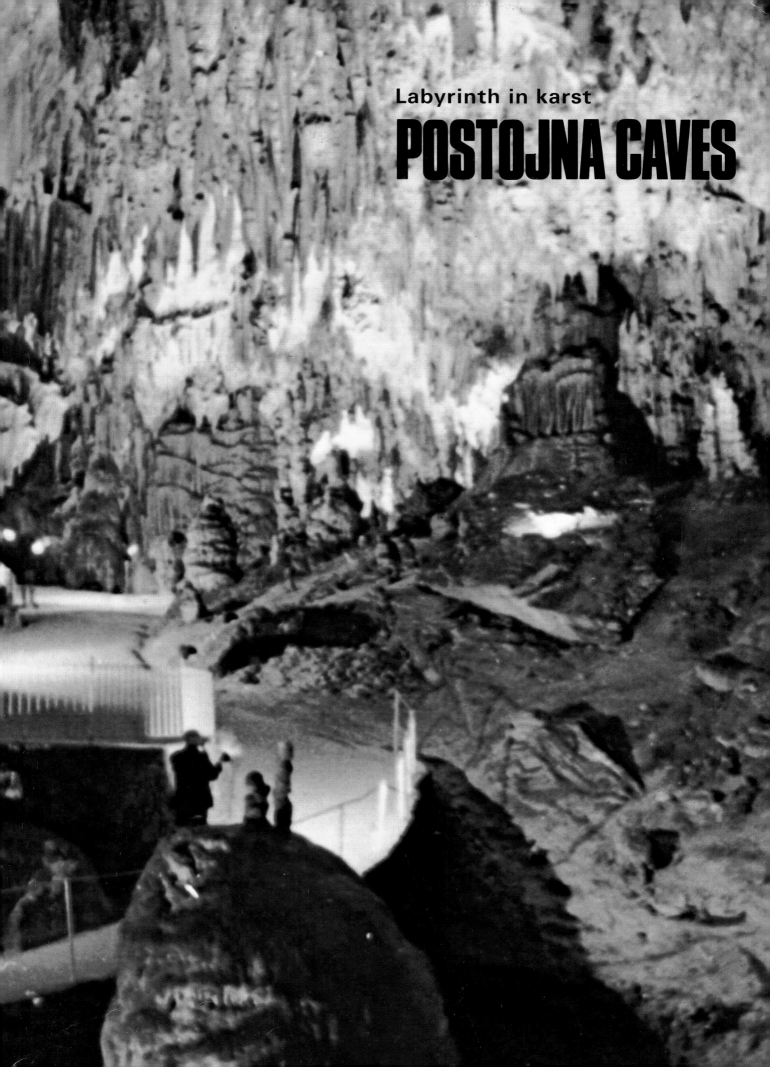

Labyrinth in karst

POSTOJNA CAVES

Phoenix out of the ashes

THE KREMLIN

KREMELIN Das Schloss in Muscau

An old Russian proverb says 'Only the Kremlin is over Moscow; over the Kremlin only the sky.' Legend has it that the first settlement on the site where Moscow now stands was founded more than 800 years ago. While hunting, Stepan Kutschka, a boyar, came across an eagle with two heads (later the heraldic beast of the Tsars) which killed a wild boar. This he took as a heavenly omen and had a small hunting village, which was named Kutschovo after him, built on the spot where this adventure had taken place. And a small village it remained until Stepan's next revelation.

The legend continues: 'In a vivid dream he saw an enormous city instead of his small village. The immense citadel with white walls and battlements stretched as far as the banks of the Nyeglinnaia. It looked unusual, the roofs resembling those which were to be found amongst the Muslims.' As a result of a toll levied by the boyar on all ships passing on the river, Kutschovo became very prosperous. This aroused the jealousy of the neighbouring Baron of Susdal, Juri Dolgoruki, who arranged to go hunting with Stepan: the next morning the boyar's body was found. He was the first victim in the Kremlin's long history of violence, intrigue and insurrection. It is doubtful if any royal fortress, even the Tower of London, was witness to as many terrible deeds as the Kremlin.

In 1325 the Metropolitan Peter moved his residence to the town on the Moskva, the 'sombre river', although at that time it was still not a place of any particular importance. The Grand Duke Ivan Danilovitch Kalita, who was recognized by the Great Khan as the ruler of Russia, had the city fortified and named the fortress Kremlin. 'Separated from the town by a fortified wall, it was a world in itself: sinister, enigmatic, the centre of power. It was here that Russian nationalism crystallized and led to the unification of the country. It was also the great stronghold of orthodox religion.'

During the course of time Moscow and the Kremlin were seized, attacked, destroyed and burned down on several occasions but time after time the citadel rose again, like the phoenix out of the ashes. He who occupies the Kremlin rules Russia: the generals of Genghis Khan, like Napoleon and Hitler, realized this, and all met disaster against the mysterious strength of this, the nucleus of Russia.

The Kremlin of Moscow (the word *Kremlin* is a general term for citadel or fortress such as were also to be found in other Russian towns) constitutes in itself a whole district of the city surrounded by a crenellated brick wall 65 feet high and $1\frac{1}{4}$ miles long, with five enormous gateways which give access to the inside. Enclosed by this wall is a whole collection of churches and monasteries, palaces and government and state buildings.

The three large cathedrals are famous. Originally erected in the fifteenth century, they were subsequently rebuilt several times. The Uspenski Cathedral (Cathedral of the Assumption), coronation church of the Tsars and burial place of earlier patriarchs, was designed by the Italian architect Fioraventi. Every time it was destroyed or plundered (in 1493, 1547, 1682 and 1812) it was rebuilt to the original plans. Facing it stands the Arkhangelski Cathedral (Cathedral of the Archangel Michael) which was designed by the Milanese architect Alevisio Novi. The Blagoveshchenski Cathedral (Cathedral of the Annunciation of the Blessed Virgin Mary) with its nine cupolas, was the church where the Tsars, to the end of the Romanov dynasty, were christened and married.

In Red Square (it was already called that before the Revolution), close to the Kremlin but outside the walls, stands the famous St Basil's Cathedral. This bizarre building, composed of eleven small interlocking chapels, was built at the command of Ivan the Terrible. Legend has it that once the cathedral had been completed the Tsar had the architect blinded so that he would never again be able to create anything of comparable splendour.

'There is no building on earth that can compare with this cathedral in its whimsical variety of shapes. In this respect no pagoda, whether in Siam, Burma or Japan, can surpass it.' (Hesse-Wartegg).

The most outstanding building in the Kremlin is the magnificent Kremlin Palace built by Thon in 1838—49 at a cost of 12,000,000 roubles. Rooms, halls, staircases, galleries and private apartments were decorated with all the splendour of imperial Russia. After the collapse of the Tsarist regime the Kremlin became the seat of the Soviet leaders and government, and the palace area, once strictly out of bounds, was opened to the public. New buildings arose in the style of the Stalinist era, while the palaces and churches were made into museums. Near the Kremlin wall a mausoleum was built for the mummified remains of Lenin which thousands of Soviet citizens file past every day. Today, as in earlier ages, the Kremlin is a symbol of power and centre of an immeasurably large realm.

Top to bottom: Kremlin Palace, seat of the Soviet leader; Zar Kolokol the largest bell in the world – it was never hung and has never sounded; entrance to the Lenin Mausoleum; golden cupolas in the Kremlin.

Left-hand page: view of Moscow with the bridge leading to Red Square, St Basil's Cathedral and the Kremlin wall (above); old general view of the 'Kremelin' in 'Muscau' (below).

Pages 98-99: St Basil's Cathedral with the 65-foot-high Kremlin wall and Red Square.

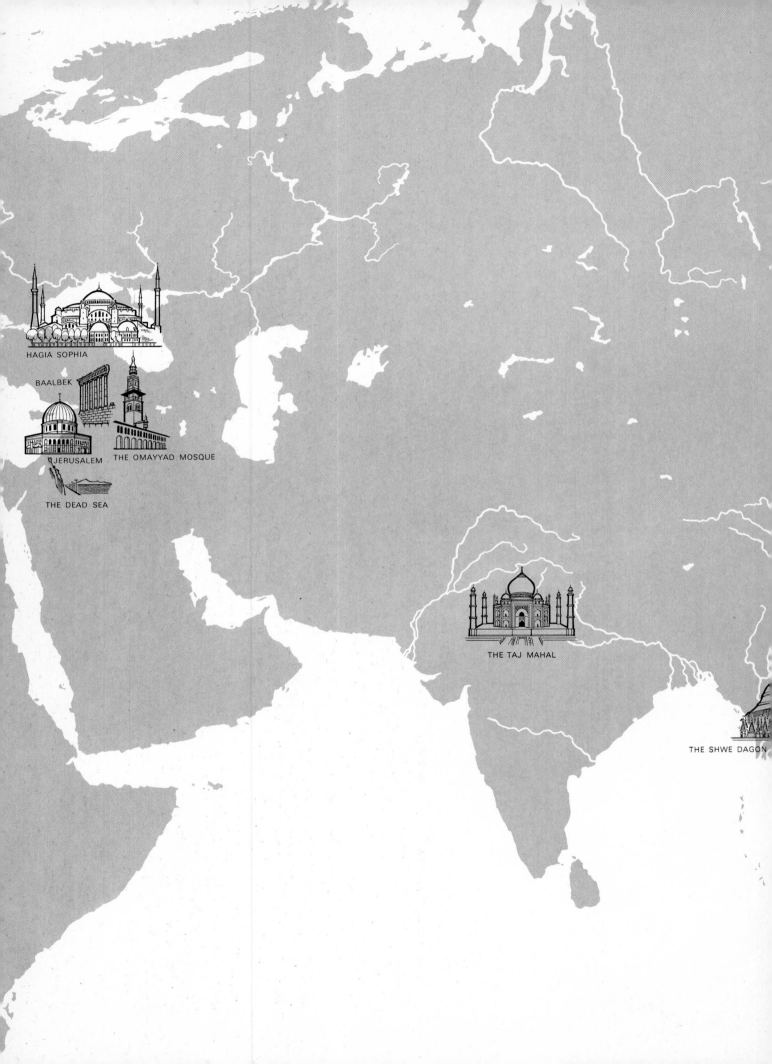

HAGIA SOPHIA

BAALBEK

JERUSALEM

THE OMAYYAD MOSQUE

THE DEAD SEA

THE TAJ MAHAL

THE SHWE DAGON

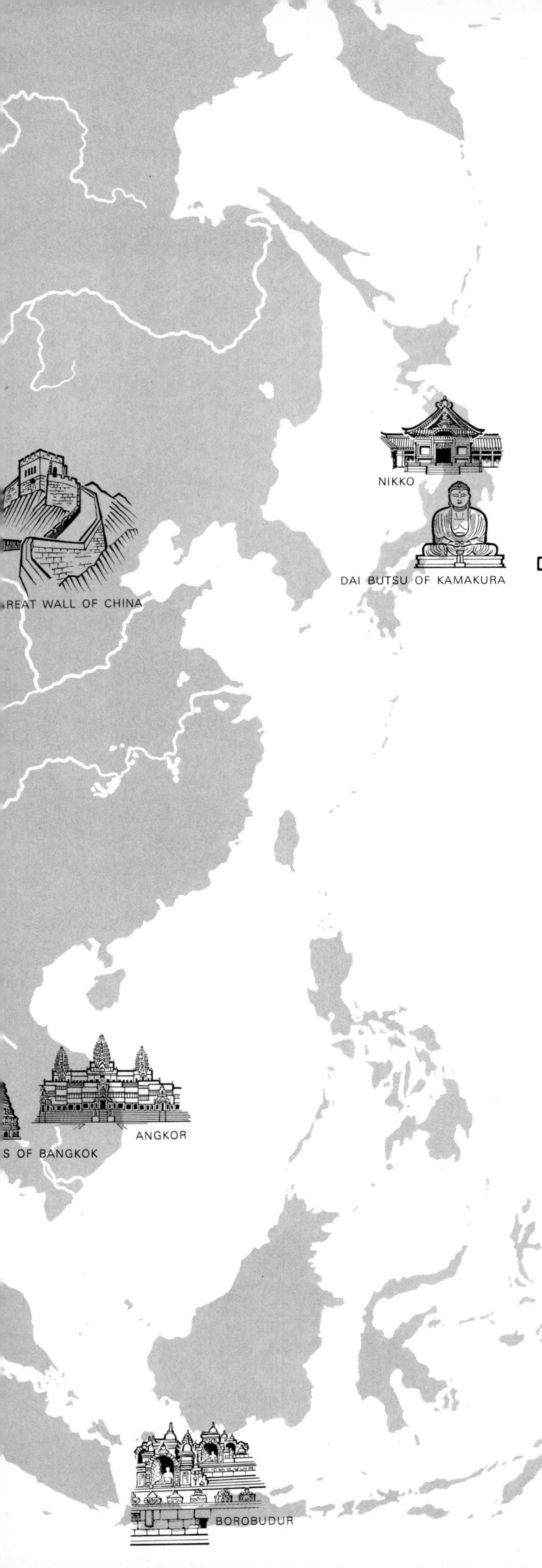

REAT WALL OF CHINA

NIKKO

DAI BUTSU OF KAMAKURA

ANGKOR

S OF BANGKOK

BOROBUDUR

WONDERS OF ASIA

The wonders of the world in the continent of Asia, apart from those in the more readily accessible Near East, have two things in common—they lie, for the most part, in countries which are rarely disturbed by the usual flow of tourist traffic and are, as a rule, religious buildings and places of worship built in bygone centuries. Not that this detracts from their grandeur—on the contrary—but it does underline the fact that modern technological achievements of the type found in other continents are still something of a novelty in Asia.

The wonders of Asia stem from history, above all from religious history. Christ, Mohammed, Buddha and Confucius all came from Asia where they were worshipped in churches, mosques and pagodas, including such buildings as the Hagia Sophia in Istanbul, the Omayyad Mosque in Damascus or the amazing temple of Borobudur in Java. In erecting these magnificent buildings everything was called upon to exhibit the power and greatness of the religion and its founder. Thus, buildings were erected which outlasted the centuries—not only outwardly, as more or less well-preserved shells, but also in the grandeur and inspiration of their conception, their architectural perfection and their uniqueness of form.

As for other sights that the countries of Asia have to offer, apart from the examples illustrated in the following pages, there are the holy cities and religious centres of Islam, especially Mecca, Karbala and Jidda, the mosques scattered from Asia Minor to India, as well as the ancient Indian temples of Ellora, Madura and a dozen other places, the Hall of the Winds in Jaipur, the pagodas of China and the Temple of Heaven in Peking. In Japan the Temple of the 33,333 Divinities in Kyoto, the prefecture of Nara and Fujiyama are of special interest. Equally, the famous Potala palace of the Dalai Lama could not be excluded from a broader selection. Even in the age of space travel the wonderland of Asia is still full of surprises.

Symbol of divine wisdom
HAGIA SOPHIA

ike a mighty fortress Hagia Sophia dominates the outline of Istanbul. For 1,500 years it has been regarded as one of the wonders of the world and admired as a unique monument to the heights of human culture.

It is difficult for the visitor today to discover behind the outward appearance of the church the lost brilliance of golden Byzantium. The changing role of Hagia Sophia—from the Christian church of churches into an Islamic mosque and finally into a museum—has left its traces behind everywhere in the form of countless alterations, additions and extensions. Only the magnificent main dome, the top of which stands 183 feet above the nave, has lost nothing of its incomparable dignity and splendour. It has been copied in the

design of countless eastern mosques and western cathedrals.

The first church on the site where Hagia Sophia now stands built by the Emperor Constantine the Great, when in 336 he m Byzantium, under the new name of Constantinople, the capital his east Roman empire. He called it *Meggale ekklesia*, the g church. Two hundred years later the building, and with it the gre part of Constantinople, went up in flames during a rebellion aga Emperor Justinian (527–56). Justinian had the church reb enlarging it and making it more beautiful than before. The p were created by Anthemius of Tralles and Isidoros of Miletus, most famous architects of Byzantium. The Emperor, however, constantly stepping in with advice and directions. 'An ange

ing him the plans for the building in his dreams,' the people pered. The building costs amounted to 360 cwt of gold.
hen finished, Hagia Sophia became the shrine of the Eastern stian church. It remained so until 1453 when the Turks seized tantinople, which ever since then has been known as Istanbul. he dismay of the Christian world the church was turned into a que and then, in 1935, Kemal Ataturk announced that it was a museum.

om the cornice of the dome stretches eastwards and west- s a semi-dome, which in its turn rests upon three small semi- es. The nave is thus covered completely by a domical canopy h, in its ascent, swells larger and larger, mounts higher and

higher, as though a miniature heaven rose overhead,' wrote Professor van Millingen. 'For lightness, for grace, for proportion, the effect is unrivalled.'

View of Hagia Sophia and the Bosphorus from the Blue Mosque in Istanbul (above right). An old etching showing what was once the most famous church in Christendom from the Schedelsch Weltchronik, 1493 (below right). The back view of Hagia Sophia testifies to the ugly accretions of the centuries (above left). Constantine the Great (centre left: the remains of his palace) built the first Great Church. Below left: representation of Christ in mosaic from the Hagia Sophia (twelfth century) Left-hand page: the interior of the church, which was transformed into a mosque.

The temples at Baalbek, intended to be larger and more magnificent than those of the Acropolis in Athens were never completed. Although, according to Arab legend, angels and spirits exerted their united powers, the temple area which lies in the Bekaa Valley between the Lebanon and the Anti-Lebanon remained unfinished. The compounded effects of wars, earthquakes and human ineptitude were such that a visitor today can see only a modest remnant of its former splendour. What he does see, however, will give him some idea of the significance that this ancient city dedicated to the sun god must once have had. The tremendous technical accomplishments of the time and the tremendous physical effort they involved are demonstrated not only by the colossal foundation stones and enormous columns at Baalbek (the highest in the ancient world), but also at the nearby quarries some ten minutes walk from the temple city on the road to Zebedani, from which builders fetched their materials. The famous block of stone still lies there just as it was left is called *Hadschar el Hubla*, 'S of the Pregnant Woman'. The intention must have been to use building the surrounding walls which, however, were never pleted. Measuring 69 feet long, 13 feet high and 16 feet wide weighing about 2,000 tons, *Hadschar el Hubla* is the la building stone in the world. No one can explain exactly how builders proposed to transport it to the site.

The Bekaa Valley was originally consecrated to Baal—hence name Baalbek. At that time there must already have been a Phoer shrine of some importance on the site where the temple ruins

Home of the sun god
BAALBEK

d, for when in the third century BC the Greek kings extended
r dominion over this part of Syria they compared the god of
lbek with the sun god worshipped by them in the Egyptian
n of Heliopolis. Moreover, Heliopolis was adopted as the new
e for Baalbek during the rule of Alexander the Great. The gods
he Phoenician era were given new names: Hadad, the god of
nder and rain, became Zeus; the nature and water goddess
rgatis was identified with the Greek goddess Aphrodite, and
god of growth and fecundity, who was just as much a part of
Baal religion, though his name has not been passed down,
renamed Hermes.
uring the centuries preceding the birth of Christ the occupants
he city changed several times. The enormous terrace on which

the remains of the Temple of Jupiter now stand must have been
built during the Seleucid period. The Seleucids were succeeded by
one of the Arab dynasties which was influenced by the Greeks and
ruled with the sanction of Rome. For five years Cleopatra ruled this
part of Syria. Finally, the city was officially incorporated into the
Roman Empire, and Augustus had it developed as an outpost.
    The Roman legionaries brought their own deities with them and

**The Temple of Bacchus at Baalbek (below), also known as the
Temple of Venus, was built outside the main temple area and has
remained virtually intact.**

once again the names of the existing gods had to be changed: Zeus became Jupiter—with the additional name of Heliopolitanus, to identify him with the city—Aphrodite was renamed Venus and Hermes was changed to Mercury. Later, when the Bacchus cult reached its peak in Rome, Bacchus mysteries were also observed in Baalbek, and a temple was specially built for the new god south of the Temple of Jupiter.

The Temple of Jupiter, once the main building of the temple precincts, extended over an area measuring 157 feet by 288 feet: it was more than twice the size of the Parthenon in Athens on which it had been modelled. Only six of the original fifty-four pillars of the Temple are still standing. Bearing a 16-foot-high entablature they stand 75 feet above the expanse of ruins like an enormous harp. Some distance away stands the better-preserved Temple of Bacchus, sometimes referred to as the Temple of Venus. Its 42-foot-high west gate is one of the most impressive creations of its kind in the world.

The enclosed area with the two enormous temples and the spacious main court decorated with 240 statues of deities was regarded as one of the wonders of the world, but even though several Roman emperors further honoured the gods by making additions to their temples, to the steps, to the surrounding walls and to the propylaea, the Acropolis of Baalbek was never finished.

The first Christian basilica is thought to have been built during the reign of Theodosius the Great (379–95) who allowed large portions of the Temple of Jupiter to be pulled down. In the year 643 a severe earthquake brought down both church and temple. Soon afterwards the Arabs took possession of Baalbek and tore down what they needed to rebuild the temple area. The impressive, well-planned Roman centre was turned into an Arab citadel—solid, strong and for centuries impregnable. The statues of the gods decayed, the columns were dismantled and for the most part carted away, many of them to adorn Byzantine basilicas and mosques.

During the centuries that followed the beauty of Baalbek faded as it became more and more disfigured. The fortress played a role in the wars of the Middle Ages, suffered in the battles of the Seljuks against the Egyptian caliph, was taken by Emir Zangi, ravaged once again by earthquakes, occupied by Saladin and stormed by the Crusaders. Much of what remained was destroyed in 1260 by Hulagu, and in 1401 when the Mongolian troops of Tamerlane advanced as far as Heliopolis.

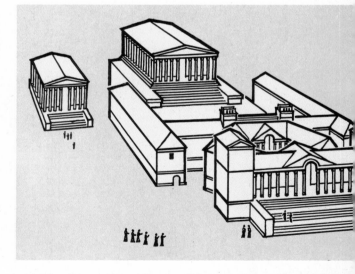

The existence of the 'Syrian Wonder' must have been known in Europe at the time of the Crusades. During the sixteenth century the demand for an excavation of the monuments steadily grew more vociferous, but nothing was done. In 1759 another earthquake severely damaged those parts of the buildings which remained intact and it was not until the beginning of the twentieth century that the reawakening of Baalbek began. The German Emperor Wilhelm II, who had been shown the ruins of ancient Heliopolis while visiting Palestine, ordered their excavation. From 1900 to 1904 German archaeologists were engaged on the work which was then continued by Lebanese experts.

The author Ernst von Khuon once observed: 'Baalbek under a violet-blue sky with delicate feathery clouds, the stone "harp" rising above the poplars of the green plain, and backed by snow-capped summits, is like a picture in a dream.'

From top to bottom: lion's head in the forecourt; columns photographed from below; reconstruction of the temple precincts; Hadschar el Hubla ('Stone of the Pregnant Woman') in the quarry near Baalbek. Right-hand page: the symbol of Baalbek – the six great columns of the Temple of Jupiter.

Wonder in Damascus

THE OMAYYAD MOSQUE

Al Dschami al Umawi, the mosque of the Omayyads—the name of this venerable building in the old town of Damascus still makes the heart of every history-conscious Arab beat faster. It reminds him of the first and most famous Arab dynasty of caliphs, the Omayyads. Even now the Bedouins enthusiastically recount tales of the heroic deeds and conquests which took place during this dynasty. The mosque built by the Omayyads in the Syrian capital is an important remnant of this illustrious chapter in Arab history. It was the centre of the declining Islamic empire, which extended over the whole of the Middle East and as far as India, the African coast of the Mediterranean and Spain. The story of the Omayyad Mosque begins with the victory of Islam over Christianity. Damascus, which the Damescenes like to describe as the oldest city on earth, has had a troubled and eventful history.

succeeded in breaking into the town from the east, whereupon Damascenes surrendered the west part of their town to Khali rival, Abu Ubayda. Their calculation paid off: the eastern part v regarded as having been defeated and was ruthlessly plunder while the western part was regarded as having been surrende and was spared. Right in the middle stood the Church of St Jo and from that time onwards it was used both by Christians a Moslems as a place of worship. In those days religious tolerar was such that the believers of both religions even used the sa entrance. It was not until seventy years later that Caliph Wali of the Omayyad dynasty negotiated with the Christians for comp possession of the church, which he wanted to turn into a magnific mosque. History books made no mention of how they reached agreement, but according to reliable sources the Christians w

It was the capital of many kingdoms and time after time it was captured, destroyed and then rebuilt again. In this city in about AD 50 St Paul was converted to Christianity, and later a group of followers of the god Jupiter was converted into one of the first Christian communities. In the third century AD the Emperor Theodosius had the temple of Jupiter in the centre of the town pulled down and replaced by a church, which was enlarged and embellished by the Emperor Justinian. It was named after St John the Baptist whose supposed head was interred there.

In AD 635 Damascus was besieged by the armies of the Islamic Arabs. The horsemen of the army commanded by Khalid ibn Walid

well compensated for the Church of St John.

The Caliph had an understanding of the arts; he wrote poe composed and played music. Under him Damascus became largest commercial and religious metropolis of the Arab wo the gate to the holy city of Mecca. During his rule the Arabs sei Spain in 711 and Samarkand in central Asia in 712.

The new mosque was to be a monument to Walid's triump First of all, the church had to be reorientated from the Christ east to face Mecca to the south. Greek architects were engaged carry out the alteration without disturbing the outer walls. The chronicles contain glowing reports of the marvellous refurnish he church. Twelve hundred artists travelled from Constantinople. most beautiful columns from decaying Roman cities were ught to Damascus for use in the building. Only the most costly rble was considered good enough to decorate the walls and ors of Walid's mosque. Golden grapevines twined round the hes of the prayer niches which were studded with precious nes. Six hundred golden lamps lit the mosque, though not for g—one of Walid I's successors had them taken down and sold. When the account for the splendid building was presented to the iph—it amounted to no less than eighteen mule loads of treasure— paid up apparently without a protest.

Of all this pomp and splendour virtually nothing is left. Countless s and the Mongol hordes of Tamerlane saw to that. In the Middle es they attacked and set fire to Damascus and plundered the

in a marble tomb covered with worn brocade, lies the supposed head of John the Baptist, who is also revered by the Moslems. One of the three minarets of the Omayyad Mosque is called *Madinet Isa*, the Jesus Minaret. According to Moslem beliefs, Jesus, revered as a prophet in Islam, will appear at the top of the minaret on the day of the Last Judgement.

The appearance of Walid I's magnificent mosque has changed but the religious ceremonies celebrated there are almost the same as when he was alive. With bowed heads the men stand in dense rows listening to the Imam's call to prayer. For thousands of years the name of Allah has sounded between the splendid pillars of the Omayyad Mosque, and the only concessions to modern technology are the powerful loudspeakers which assist the Imam and the muezzins on the minarets.

ayyad mosque. In 1893 a disastrous fire destroyed all that re- ned. Today the most precious items in the Omayyad mosque the 3,000 rugs which cover the greater part of the marble r. Some of them are extremely beautiful and hundreds of years Everything else of course, is of antique design but dates from r the great fire in 1893. The mosque itself consists of a long angular central building flanked by two smaller rectangular gs. The prayer room, which is also the main room, is 446 feet g and 88 feet wide and lined by two rows of Corinthian columns. the centre there is a small chapel with a domed roof, and den railings between the slender marble pillars. Inside, encased

Exterior of the Omayyad Mosque (above) with the large court-yard. Left-hand page: colonnade along the façade of the Mosque (left); tomb of John the Baptist (above right); treasury (below right).

Pages 112–113: interior with carpeted floor.

115

Holy city of three religions
JERUSALEM

The name sometimes given to Jerusalem 'Princess of Peace' is bitterly ironical. For this city, the scene of the Passion, the death and Resurrection of Jesus Christ, there has been no peace for two thousand years. In no other holy city in the world has blood flowed so freely. Nowhere has more bitter fighting, deeper hatred, been seen as in the little town in the barren, grey hills of Judaea. For three world religions—Islam, Judaism and Christianity have fought for possession of Jerusalem.

Yet nowhere have so many prayers been said as in Jerusalem for, as the author Peter Bamm explained: 'The cause of the strife over Jerusalem was always an excess of one virtue—the virtue of piety.' Since the time of Christ the city has been captured eleven times and completely destroyed on five occasions. Yet its ruins continue to harbour memories of the past, even though, according to archaeologists, biblical Jerusalem lies under a 65 foot layer of rubble. It is, therefore, uncertain whether tourists today really want to rediscover Jerusalem as it really was two thousand years ago.

In the year AD 70 the legions of Titus set fire to Jerusalem. The area in a ten mile circle round the town was deforested and as a result it degenerated into the chalky desert that it is today. The triple city wall was torn down, the temple of the Jews plundered and destroyed. The few remains were completely demolished by the Romans when the Jews under Ben Kochba—his name is known from the Dead Sea Scrolls—tried to expel the Roman oppressors. A new city, Aelia Capitolina, founded by Hadrian, was built on top of the rubble. Two hundred years later the pious Empress Helena journeyed from Byzantium to look for the holy sites. She searched for and found the Holy Sepulchre. From that time onwards Jerusalem was a constant centre of conflict and strife. In the year 614 it was destroyed by the Persians; in 637 it was captured by Caliph Omar, by the Seljuks in 1072, by the Crusaders in 1099. In 1187 Sultan Saladin recaptured the city from the French knights; in 1617 the Ottoman Turks stormed the city walls; in 1917 a British army entered Jerusalem.

Since 1948 Jordan and Israel have quarrelled bitterly over possession of the Holy City. Under pressure from the United Nations an armistice was agreed upon, each adversary retaining precisely that part of the city which it occupied, and a border just as absurd as it was arbitrary was established. A deserted strip of no-man's-land marked by barbed wire bisected what for thousands of years had been a whole. A single entrance linked the two Jerusalems: the Mandelbaum Gate. The Jordanians would not allow the Jews to pray at the Wailing Wall, the great shrine of the Jewish people. This wall is the only part of the temple remaining after the city was destroyed by the Romans. It consists of enormous blocks of stone measuring as much as 36 feet by 16 feet. Eleven rows of blocks are hidden by rubble but fourteen are still visible. Since Israel's attack on the Sinai Peninsula in June 1967 and its seizure of the old city

View of the city from the Dominus Flevit chapel showing the gilded dome of the Dome of the Rock, the monument to Mohammed's ascension.

117

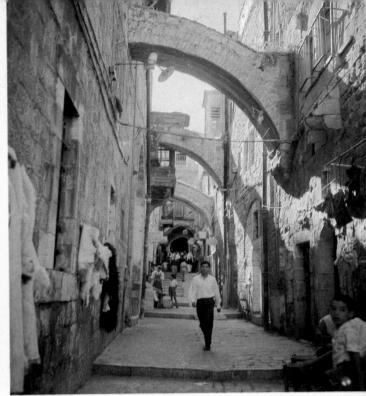

of Jerusalem, pious Jews have been able to pray at the Wailing Wall. On Fridays and feast days grey-bearded men kiss the stones, cry and bewail the destruction of the temple. Whether future generations of Jews will be able to kneel before the Wailing Wall no one can say, for the tragedy of the Holy City has still not come to an end.

The Christian monuments in Jerusalem have suffered the same misfortunes as the Jewish ones. To Christians Mount Calvary with the Holy Sepulchre is the most important place of pilgrimage in Jerusalem. After passing through a labyrinth of tiny twisting streets one is suddenly confronted by the romanesque façade of the Church of the Holy Sepulchre. It makes a scruffy, dilapidated impression. All the architectural styles of the last thousand years are represented there. The unsuspecting visitor is surprised to encounter Islam at the entrance: according to an ancient right the door keepers of the church are a Muslim family.

In the centre, in a garland of chapels which all relate to Christian history, lies the chapel containing the Tomb. Another chapel is built over the rock of Golgotha. A depression framed in silver in-

dicates where the cross is said to have stood. Under the chur dome stands a small marble chapel with an anteroom, the so-call Angel's Chapel, containing the stone which the angels rolled aw from Christ's grave. Behind it lies the Holy Sepulchre itself, a ti room with space for no more than four people. A smell of incen pervades the air. The chamber is lit by forty-three valuable lam belonging to the different Christian denominations. The walls a lined with marble. Pilgrims kneel in prayer before the stone which the body of the Redeemer is said to have lain.

Five denominations—Greek Orthodox, Roman Catholic, Syri Coptic and Jacobitic—a small Syrian congregation—share cont of the church. They jealously guard the chapels, lamps and donatio At the tomb itself they replace each other according to a fin timed rota and keep a sharp lookout to ensure that nobody puts offering into the plate of the wrong denomination.

It required scholarly detective work to determine the exact loc tion of the holy places in a city which had suffered so much destru tion. In the case of the Church of the Holy Sepulchre there is s some disagreement as to whether it was actually built over t

gotha hill and the grave of Joseph of Arimathea. The debris of
[th]e weighs all too heavily on the past.
[I]t is well known that the Via Dolorosa, the street along which
[Jes]us had to carry His cross, has changed its location more than
[onc]e. The street which now bears this name, a narrow little alley,
[is] merely a symbol of pious memory. Signs indicate the fourteen
[sta]tions of the Cross. The first lies near the convent of the French
[sis]ters of Zion, the fourteenth and last is the tiny chapel of the
[tom]b in the Church of the Holy Sepulchre.
[I]t is difficult to discover the town of Jesus Christ in the Jerusalem
[of] today. The general turmoil, the commercialization of the holy
[pla]ces are frequently repugnant. Only in the Garden of Gethsemane
[at t]he foot of the Mount of Olives can one find a scene as peaceful
[no]w as it was two thousand years ago when Jesus sat there with
[His] disciples. The garden now belongs to the Franciscans, charged
[by] the Pope with guarding this holy place.
[F]rom the Garden of Gethsemane there is an extensive view of the
[city] with its tortuous walls. On Palm Sunday Jesus, seated on a
[don]key, entered Jerusalem through the Golden Gate in the city

wall amid the people's cries of 'Hosannah!' Up to the eighth century
the Greek patriarch of Jerusalem rode into the city every year through
the Golden Gate, but it was then bricked up by the Arabs who were
afraid of an old prophecy which said that a Christian conqueror
was to enter Jerusalem through this gate.
    Jerusalem, however, is a holy city not only for Christians and
Jews; it is also revered by the Moslems as the third holiest city of
Islam after Mecca and Medina, for it was from Jerusalem that
Mohammed is said to have ascended into Paradise on the winged
mare Burak. The place where this is said to have happened, the
Haram al Sharif on Mount Moria was also venerated by the Jews,

**Top row from left: Church of Christ's Nativity in Bethlehem; Via
Dolorosa in Jerusalem; view of the Church of the Holy Sepulchre;
Stabat Mater altar in the Church of the Holy Sepulchre.
Bottom row from left: tree in the Garden of Gethsemane; columns
in the Church of the Holy Sepulchre; the 'Place where Pilate arrested
[sic] and flogged Jesus'; paving stones in front of the Church of
the Holy Sepulchre.**

LOCUS IN QUO
APPREHENDIT PILATUS JESUM
ET FLAGELLAVIT.

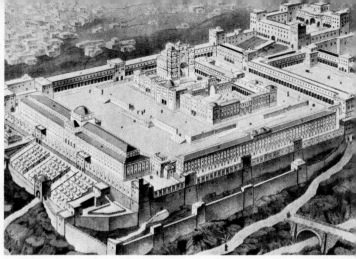

for King David had erected a sacrificial altar on the crumbling rock. On the same site Solomon built the first Jewish temple in about 960 BC. Under protest from the Jews the Arabs also constructed an enormous monument here to commemorate Mohammed's ascension. Known as the Dome of the Rock, it became the symbol of Jerusalem. Contrary to what is said in many tourist guides, the Dome of the Rock was never used as a mosque, nor is the much-used title Mosque of Omar correct. With its gilded dome, it was always intended as a shrine to mark the holy rock, and religious services were never held there. For this purpose an attractive mosque, the

Aqsa Mosque, was built at the south-eastern corner.

The Dome of the Rock is reached from all sides by eight stairw ending in arcades, called *Mawazin*, the 'balances', by the Ara According to Islamic legend, a horse hair will be hung from 'balances' to the Mount of Olives on the Day of Judgement. those risen from the dead must walk across it and anyone who sinned will fall into eternal damnation. In the Dome of the Ro the guide shows mementos of Mohammed's ascension on hor back: the archangel Gabriel left a fingerprint in the stone; winged horse a hoof mark as it prepared to take off. A depress

e rock was made by the prophet's turban: he was rising from
er and would have banged his head if the rock had not suddenly
me soft and given way.

row from left: Jews at the Wailing Wall; reconstruction of the
dian temple; old picture of Jerusalem; the Mount of Olives
the city. Below: view of the Old Town of Jerusalem with the
e of the Rock, left centre.

'A suicide who chose death by drowning,' wrote M. Y. Ben-gavriêl, 'would not be able to carry out his plan in the Dead Sea, for the water which consists of up to 25 per cent magnesium chloride, calcium chloride and sodium chloride, would prevent his body sinking. Salt will no longer dissolve in this water, in which no fish stirs and no crustacean can live.'

According to the account in the Bible, the towns of Sodom and Gomorrah sank in the waters of the 'Salt Sea' during a terrifying rain of fire and brimstone. The angels informed only two inhabitants of Sodom of the impending disaster: they were Lot, son of Haran and nephew of Abraham, and his wife. Both were allowed to flee in time—but only on condition that neither looked round while they were making their escape. Lot's wife could not resist the temptation to do so and was turned into a pillar of salt. This story is also related in the Koran, and the Arab name for the Dead Sea is *Bahret Lut*, Lot Lake.

In fact the Dead Sea is not a sea at all but a lake with an area of 380 square miles. Its surface lies 1,292 feet below sea level, and it is the lowest depression in the world. It is fed principally by the River Jordan, of which it is the outlet, and it has never been connected to the open sea. The 2,601 foot deep trough was probably formed between the Tertiary and Quarternary periods and filled with water during the Ice Age.

Today, the Dead Sea is an international tourist centre with modern hotels springing up along its shores. At the same time it is a major source of minerals, and factories make full use of the water's high salt content. The discovery, in the ruins at Qumran on the north-west shore, of the Dead Sea Scrolls containing texts from the Old Testament and writings of the Essene community at Qumran, has added further fame to this historically important region.

High above the Dead Sea (in the foreground a potash basin) stands the 'Rock of Lot's Wife' (right-hand page). From top to bottom: the place of Christ's baptism in the Jordan; bush choked with salt; bathing in front of the Dead Sea Casino; sign giving details of altitude.

The lowest lake on earth
THE DEAD SEA

Memorial to a great love

THE TAJ MAHAL

It is said that on seeing the marble splendour of the Taj Mahal an eminent Englishwoman once sighed, 'What I think I cannot say, but I feel that I would like to die tomorrow, if my bones were to be covered by such a monument.'

This marble mausoleum was commissioned by Shah Jahan, the fifth emperor of the Mogul dynasty, who reigned from 1628 to 1658. His ascent to the throne was not achieved without overcoming obstacles. Before he could install himself in office, he had to dispose of all his kinsmen and send his mother into banishment. So much the greater, therefore, was the love he showed for his wife, whom he honoured with the name of Mumtaz-i-Mahal, 'Jewel of the Palace'. On the banks of the Jumna near Agra, Shah Jahan constructed a garden paradise for his wife. Marble pathways led through an oasis planted with exotic flowers and trees for, according to an old report, 'Nothing was to harm the little bare feet of the delicate princess when she walked there.

The great Mogul had a sense of the magnificent. He not only had superb buildings erected in Agra, but also filled his residence at Delhi with mosques and palaces of breathtaking beauty. An inscription in the reception chamber of his great imperial fort in Delhi, in which the legendary Peacock Throne is said to have stood, proudly proclaims in Persian: 'If there is a paradise on earth, then it is this, then it is this, then it is this!'

In spite of the lasting monuments the Mogul Emperor created in the form of countless works of art, he is remembered by posterity not as the person who re-shaped Delhi, which was to be called Jahanabad after him, but as the man responsible for building the Taj Mahal. In this building lie the remains of the ruler who controlled a large part of India. But the end of his reign was as inauspicious as its beginning. Shah Jahan was deposed by his son Aurangzeb and imprisoned in the palace, 'where he led a dissolute life of pleasure until his death .

124

After the death of Aurangzeb the empire began to crumble.

Shah Jahan's favourite wife, Mumtaz-i-Mahal, who is said to have exerted great influence on the Emperor through her beauty and intelligence, bore the ruler of India seven children. In 1629, after the birth of her eighth child, she died in southern Indian of puerperal fever. The Mogul had her body brought home to Agra and buried in the gardens on the River Jumna. Above her grave the Emperor built a tomb like nothing the world had ever seen before. 'The overwhelming impression that the Taj Mahal exercises on the beholder depends essentially upon the effects of contrast. The sparkling strip of water with its lotus flowers which leads from the entrance gate through the gardens up to the Taj Mahal, the proud building of snow-w marble, the luxuriant green of the grounds which surround it, the deep blue of the Indian sky above—all this combines to fo picture that for a moment makes all the cares and needs of ea existence disappear from the soul of the beholder, and this o whelming effect does not readily find an equal in the world.' (Deussen).

Some people have called this 'dream in marble' an 'apothe of Indian womanhood'. Shah Jahan gathered round him the famous architects and craftsmen to prepare the design of building. The construction of the dome was probably the

sibility of an expert from Istanbul; the masons came from Delhi
Kandahar; specialists were brought from Lahore and Samarkand
uild the pinnacle on the dome; the calligraphers for the inlaid
iptions travelled from Shiraz and Baghdad, the flower carvers
Bukhara, the landscape gardener from Kashmir. For seventeen
20,000 workers were engaged on the construction of what is
ably the most famous tomb in the world. The building costs
been estimated at £6,250,000.

Karl Baedeker's opinion: 'The general impression exceeds all
ctations. The simplicity of the design and the perfection of its
ution combine to form a miracle of art which for sublime beauty

can compete with the temples of the Greeks and the most famous
cathedrals of the Middle Ages and the Renaissance.'

**Above: interior of the Taj Mahal with the marble tombs of Shah
Jahan and his favourite wife, Mumtaz-i-Mahal (foreground).
Left-hand page: entrance gate to the Taj Mahal (above left); part
of the façade of the gate (above right); one of the windows worked
in marble filigree (below left); floral relief in marble (below right).**

ity of 400 shrines

THE TEMPLES OF BANGKOK

The 17,000 Buddhist shrines in Thailand (Siam) surpass all other temples that the Far East has to offer. Thailand's temples are colourful, gay and spectacular, and the most beautiful of all are the 400-odd in its capital, Bangkok, on the River Menam. In 1785 Rama I, an ancestor of the present king founded the royal palace and temple city. In those days the temple area occupied a fifth of the total area of the new capital and even now it still forms the heart of this city of 2,000,000 inhabitants. The fantastic world of Buddhist myth lives on in the names of Bangkok's temples, one of the most splendid of which is Wat Po, the 'Temple of the Holy Fig Tree'. It gets its name from the fig tree growing in one of the walls, beneath which Buddha is said to have gained enlightenment. In fact Wat Po is a temple town in itself—a maze of halls, chapels, towers, terraces and monks' cells, in which one would be hopelessly lost without a guide. There is a gallery of 394 statues of Buddha in Wat Po, but also a colossal 160 foot long gilded statue of the Reclining Buddha.

Figures with fierce demonic expressions keep watch over all the temples in Bangkok, including Wat Phra Kaeo, the Temple of the Emerald Buddha, the most magnificent of all the shrines in Bangkok. Inside, behind doors of costly ebony, stands a 31-inch-high statue of Buddha carved out of jade, the head of which consists of a single enormous emerald. This smiling figure is Thailand's national icon. In accordance with an ancient ritual the king enters the temple three times a year in order to change the jewelled garments of the figure. The winter dress envelops both the Buddha's shoulders; the summer dress leaves them free; and at the beginning of the fruitful rainy season the Emerald Buddha is dressed in a garment of pure gold which covers just one shoulder.

Temples of Bangkok: Wat Arun (above), Wat Benchamabopitr (centre left) and Wat Phra Kaeo (centre right). Below left: head of the Reclining Buddha in Wat Po. Below right: guards modelled on the Italian traveller, Marco Polo. Left-hand page: gold statues in Wat Phra Kaeo.

Pages 128-129: Wat Phra Kaeo.

The most beautiful of all Buddhist temples is also the home of the most highly treasured Buddhist relics. Under the enormous dome of the Shwe Dagon Pagoda in Rangoon, in shrines glittering with jewels, lie eight of Buddha's hairs. Anyone standing in front of the golden 'Cathedral of Buddhism' for the first time can appreciate why, compared with this, the seven wonders of the ancient world seemed so modest to the first travellers to Asia. Like a glowing mountain of gold the 550 foot main pagoda (it is 45 feet higher than Cologne Cathedral) towers above the Burmese capital. In the case of the Shwe Dagon Pagoda all that glitters really is gold. For that King Mindon Min, a particularly generous Burmese ruler, was responsible. In 1871 he had the main dome of the largest shrine in his kingdom of rice farmers covered with pure gold at a cost of something like £4,500,000. The tip of the shrine is studded with thousands of precious stones: rubies, emeralds and diamonds. Right at the top, below the graceful parasol-shaped tower, 100 gold and 1,400 silver bells of various sizes rock gently in the wind.

Europeans can only stare in amazement at this unheard-of wealth. It is, however, not so much an ostentatious gesture of opulence, as the expression of a spiritual attitude characteristic of Buddhism: the material treasures of this world are subordinate to the spiritual ones. There is nothing exceptional about the splendour of the Shwe Dagon Pagoda. All the pagodas in Burma were donated by men as pious as they were rich, and today it is still customary for rich Burmese to build a pagoda when they near the end of their life. Almost all these temples have golden walls and jewelled spires which reflect the sun's rays. The donor gains special spiritual merit if the pagoda he builds is erected on an artificial mound. The Shwe Dagon Pagoda stands on a specially constructed 180-foot-high platform of earth, and the temple encompasses a total area of about 75,000 square yards—something like the size of the square of Cologne Cathedral.

As a token of respect pilgrims take off their shoes at the foot of the terraced mound. Barefoot they file along the four covered market streets which lead to the shrine. Here, amid the colourful crowded market scene, the atmosphere is not one of particular solemnity. Street traders sell offerings, lotus blooms, bowls of rice and small bundles of gold leaf. There is always a ready market for gold leaf and many families save for years in order to buy some. Their faces radiant with joy, they carefully stick it to the walls of the main pagoda or to the dozens of pagodas and small temples which have been built around it during the course of time. The

THE SHWE DAGON PAGODA

gold shrine of Shwe Dagon will never fade!

The temples in Burma are ogee- or bell-shaped buildings and not in the least reminiscent of the Thai temples with their terraced roofs. The Shwe Dagon Pagoda is a classic example of Burmese temple building. Dome-shaped buildings of this kind are known as stupas. Underneath their mantle of gold they are made of bricks so solidly packed together that there is not the smallest gap between them. Legend has it that a king once had a master-builder executed because he discovered a hole no bigger than a pinhead between the bricks of his pagoda. The Burmese believe that a mystic relationship exists between a pagoda and the body of the person who commissions it so that every mistake in its construction is followed by illness in its patron. The dome shape of the stupas derives from ancient Burmese history. The Burmese originally came from the border land between China and Tibet and moved into what is now Burma during the ninth century AD. At that time they were not Buddhists but worshipped the Nats, a goblin-type race of tree and river spirits. The statues of the two most powerful Nats were kept on Mount Popa, a cone-shaped volcano abounding in flowers and known as the Golden Mountain or Mountain of Flowers. The memory of this holy mountain is preserved in the golden stupas of Burma.

The Burmese did not want to part with their Nats, and the Shwe Dagon Pagoda is guarded at every corner and crossing by delightful statues of these spirits and fairies, who, it is believed, still float in the air and affect the destinies of the people. The bells on the temple terrace, which hang there by the hundred, are struck in order to attract their attention. On the north-eastern side of the terrace one of the largest bells in the world, weighing over 20 tons, hangs in a gilded pagoda. Between the carefree Nats sit hundreds of earnest-looking Buddhas made of alabaster, clay or marble. Seven of them are named after the seven planets, and men, women and children carefully set down offerings in front of the Buddha under whose sign they were born. Deep in prayer, they kneel before the statues, the women always slightly behind the men. A travel writer once described the enormous temple square of the Shwe Dagon Pagoda as 'an oriental Acropolis'. It is one of the spiritual centres of the Buddhist world. The atmosphere is pervaded by the collected calm of meditation as absorbed in discussion about the

Many small auxiliary pagodas surround the 550-foot-high golden Shwe Dagon Pagoda in the Burmese capital.

133

teachings of Buddha, monks clad in saffron yellow wander back and forth between the temples.

Occasionally the toll of a bell sounds across the golden rooftops, but apart from that the silence of the golden pagoda is broken only by the murmur of the monks as they expound philosophical doctrines to keenly attentive young men.

Richly embellished sacred buildings near the Shwe Dagon Pagoda (above). Right-hand page: a street of temples in Rangoon (above); foot of the Shwe Dagon Pagoda (below left); temple guards, 65 feet high.

The fairytale city in the jungle
ANGKOR

In 1858 the world was astounded by the news contained in a report by the French naturalist, Henri Mouhout. He had, he said, discovered a temple in the middle of the jungle in Cambodia which was more magnificent than anything that had been found in Greece or Rome. This temple, known as Angkor Wat, could only be compared with the Temple of Solomon and must have been built by some eastern Michelangelo.

It was soon discovered that Angkor Wat was by no means unique but in fact formed part of an enormous complex of temples and palaces which had been constructed during the period AD 800 to AD 1200 and covered an area of almost thirty square miles. Later it became evident that there must once have been thousands of temples in the jungle of Cambodia, 'a whole primeval forest of carved stones' erected by the Khmer.

A great deal was learned about the Khmer from the inscriptions at Angkor. At its peak the Khmer empire not only extended over present-day Cambodia but also covered parts of Thailand, Laos, Burma and Vietnam. Rice formed the basis of their diet and in order to increase the number of crops a year they built immense reservoirs, known as *barays*— two of them with a capacity of about 2,000,000,000 gallons were found in Angkor alone. Their kings were regarded as divine. Consequently, most of the temples were not houses of god in the sense of our churches but temple-palaces inaccessible to the people. Night after night in the temple tower of Angkor Wat a mystic marriage took place between the king and the soul of a nine-headed snake which appeared to him in the form of a woman. The temple-mountain of Baphuon, a pyramid-like structure, was built in about 1050. This relatively modest building was later incorporated into the precincts of Angkor Thom. The magnificent temple area of Angkor Wat was built during the reign of Suryavarman II (1113–46). The Khmer, who were Hindus, dedicated this religious centre to Vishnu. Constructed as a mountain of temples, it symbolizes the centre of the universe. The outer wall encloses a rectangle measuring over 3,000 feet long and 2,500 feet wide and is crowned by five towers. A maze of paths and terraces with countless sculptures served as the home for the god-king and the Hindu gods. Only the lowest gallery, decorated with bas-reliefs of various religious scenes, was open to the people.

Some decades later, during the reign of Jayavarman VII (1181–1220), the

Dozens of gigantic stone heads decorate the Khmer temple ruins at Angkor Thom.

city of Angkor Thom with the Bayon temple area was built close to Angkor Wat. Unlike his predecessors, Jayavarman was a Buddhist. The imperial temple of Bayon, therefore, was dedicated to Buddha, while at the same time demonstrating the power of the king. There were fifty-two rectangular towers decorated with stone heads up to eight feet high looking towards the four quarters of the sky. Over 200 of these stone faces have been counted. Their expression corresponds to that of future Buddhas (Bodhisattvas) and it is thought that the king's face was probably used as a model.

Angkor is the most extensive temple area in Asia. Hundreds of other temples covered with reliefs and sculptures were found in the tropical forest surrounding Angkor Wat and Angkor Thom, evidence of the flourishing Khmer civilization.

their temple city all the more inexplicable. There are dozens of the as to why Angkor (in English 'the town') was deserted by it habitants. Did the vital water supply fail? Did the hostile Cha Thais invade the rich country? Did the god-kings exhaust thems with their endless temple building? Were there religious reas Did the land cease to bear rice?

As there are no written records of what happened, the true re will probably never be ascertained. Locked for ever in the 'su city of petrified fantasy' the secret will remain.

Around the year 1000 Angkor, with a population of over one million, must have been the largest city in the world, larger even than Rome. Over the past century French archaeologists have uncovered the walls overgrown by tropical vegetation and have reconstructed many of the temples. Many conclusions about the history of the Khmer could be drawn from the inscriptions, but at the same time several mysteries emerged which were only solved in the course of time. The greatest enigma of all is what caused the collapse of Angkor.

The Khmer undoubtedly had astonishing artistic and technical abilities which makes the fact that in the year 1432 they abandoned

Above left: stone carving on the Terrace of Elephants at An Thom. Above: colossal head in the Bayon, the main temple Angkor Thom. Right-hand page, left row from above: round-e demons on the approach road to Angkor Thom – they are one sid a long double row of sculptures illustrating the myth of the Chur of the Ocean of Milk; statue of the 'leprous king' and seven-hea god, both in Angkor Thom; walls overgrown by tropical vegeta (Angkor Wat). Above right: bas-relief of battle scene in Angkor V Below right: central building of Angkor Wat with approach ro

Japan's most famous temple town
NIKKO

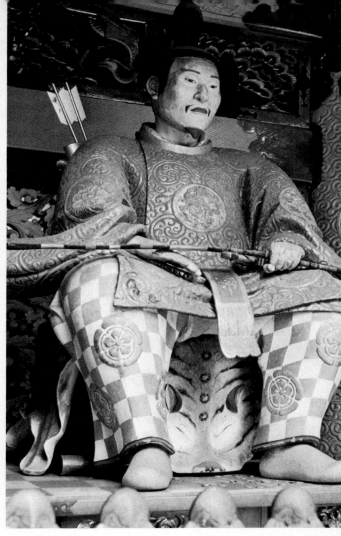

hen the great shogun Ieyasu of the line of the Tokugawa closed his eyes for ever, his last wish was fulfilled and he was laid to rest in the mountain district of Nikko, sixty miles from the new capital, Edo, at that time still a poor fishing village, which, many years later would develop into a city with a population of millions, Tokyo. Ieyasu had succeeded in defeating his rival princes, in conquering several provinces and in laying the foundations for a united Japanese empire. It was an empire in which Ieyasu as shogun (roughly, a commander-in-chief of the empire) and as the real ruler in place of the powerless emperor, headed a powerful, authoritarian regime.

In 1617 the dead statesman and warrior was interred at N among the gods. In the dramatic scenery of Nikko—now a Japa National Park—numerous buildings were erected in his ho Gates, pagodas and shrines were built; gradually, a whole con of temples arose. At first the area was dedicated to Buddha; it served the simpler Shinto cult, the native religion of Japan. Le has it that a work force of 830,000 people built the magnif Toshogu shrine within a period of fifteen months. Iemitsu, the gr son and second successor to Ieyasu, was also buried at N with divine honours. The temple area developed into a m frequented place of pilgrimage, and while the richer pilgrims dor

ze or stone offertory lamps in honour of the great shoguns, the
er ones planted a tree or handed over a few small coins to the
ts. As in all great Shinto temples in Japan, there was a court with
pen stage on which a graceful young priestess performed
ous dances.
n passing through the Niomon Gate one comes to the stable of
acred grey horses. The spirits of the great shoguns may go for
e whenever they like. A wood carving over the stable door
cts three monkeys which signify by the position of their hands:
r no evil, speak no evil, see no evil.' It is the original of that group
onkeys so often seen in the West on writing desks or cabinets.

The monkeys of Nikko must be some of the most often copied
animals in history.
  The Japanese say: 'Nikko wo minai utschi wa, kekko to yu na!'
'Don't say "magnificent" until you've seen Nikko!'

**Above: colourful gable of the Toshogu shrine in Nikko. Left-hand
page: offertory lanterns in Nikko (above left); temple guard with
bow and arrows (above right); detail from the Toshogu shrine
(below left); the famous monkeys of Nikko – hear no evil, speak no
evil, see no evil (below right). Pages 140-141: Yomeimon Gate
and Toshogu shrine, Nikko.**

143

The 700-year-old giant Buddha

DAI BUTSU OF KAMAKURA

'We went through the gate,' says a nineteenth-century traveller's report, 'and the imposing image of the god towered in front of us in impenetrable calm, a work of art of the first order, created 600 years ago. There is a majesty about the whole gigantic figure which is difficult to describe. The concept of omnipotent power, self-contained, absolute and therefore without emotion, is masterfully expressed in the posture and face of the Buddha seated in still, regal dignity and looking down through half-closed eyes.'

The gigantic Buddha of Kamakura in Japan has a similar impact on travellers today. The Japanese say, and they are right, that he shows his real face at sunset. In the half-light of dusk the giant bronze Buddha radiates most clearly the tranquility of a transcendent being, the security of being impervious to temporal influences. The man standing like a dwarf before the forty-five-foot-high giant is aware of a sense of timelessness.

There are two colossal statues of the Gautama Buddha, known by the Japanese as Butsu, on Japanese soil. The older one is in the Todaiji monastery at Nara and is fifty-two feet high. It owes its existence to a pledge by the emperor. It is known that 18,656 cords of charcoal were used in casting the statue, that the gilding took 10,446 ounces of gold and that Kuninaka no Muraji Kimimaro, the grandson of a Chinese immigrant, was responsible for the work. But no one now knows what this Dai Butsu originally looked like. In the course of time it was partially destroyed and has been repaired on four occasions.

Of the original figure only the legs, crossed in the lotus position, remain. In its present form the figure itself, which dates from between 1701 and 1708, is regarded by one art historian as a 'dreadful and ridiculous caricature'.

The Dai Butsu of Nara is, in a manner of speaking, the father of the bronze Buddha of Kamakura. Minamoto no Yoritomo, the first of the Japanese shoguns, whom the people called the 'greatest conqueror of the barbarians', prevailed against his rivals and in 1185 he took over the administration of the country. Under his rule learning and the arts flourished. This period is known in the history of Japanese art as the Kamakura epoch.

Minamoto no Yoritomo proposed to break the predominance of Nara as the cultural centre—even now this town is often referred to as a Buddhist Rome. This entailed building a statue of Buddha of equal standing to the Dai Butsu of Nara, and the task was assigned to the sculptor, Ono Goroemon. By 1252 the casting was complete, and with that Kamakura, for one and a half centuries (1192–1333), the seat of the shogunate had also demonstrated its commanding role in the realm of the arts.

The statue of the giant Buddha seated in the lotus position is mounted on a terraced platform approached by a flight of steps. The bronze parts from which the statue was assembled are up to four inches thick. The face alone is nine feet long; the distance from knee to knee is thirty-six feet.

At one time the Dai Butsu was housed in a sort of hall like the Buddha of Nara. Temples and palaces were built round the shrine. In the course of time fires and typhoons reduced all these wooden buildings to rubble and ashes. The capital, Kamakura, once a proud metropolis, with a population numbered in the hundreds of thousands, did not survive the Japanese Middle Ages. The only evidence of its former greatness is the Dai Butsu which since 1495 has stood exposed to the sky. The bronze has gradually weathered to a blackish green.

The German traveller, P. G. Heims, visited Kamakura just before the turn of the century. In front of the terrace below the base of the Dai Butsu he found an entrance gate which was flanked by enormous guards in the form of hideously grotesque red idols. The red lacquer was covered with countless white blots. Heims discovered the cause: 'Anyone who comes here to ask for something from the idols writes his request on a piece of paper which is then chewed and spat at the idols. If it adheres, the request is accepted. Some have managed to catapult their requests as far as the brows of the faces.'

Heims covered the distance from Tokyo to Kamakura, a journey of thirty miles or more, by rickshaw. A coolie pulled from the front; a second pushed from behind. It must have been a laborious journey. Today an electric express train goes from Tokyo to Kamakura. For the inhabitants of Tokyo a visit to the statue of Buddha is a Sunday outing, though an even greater attraction, perhaps, is the nearby 'Japanese Riviera', Sagami Bay, a popular holiday resort.

The face of the enormous Buddha is nine feet long (below). It is possible to see inside through the windows in the back (right). The hands (below right) are placed together in meditation. The Buddha statue made of individual pieces of bronze (right-hand page) is 45 feet high.
Pages 144–145: visitors to Kamakura are dwarfed by the great Dai Butsu.

A monument to blood and tears

THE GREAT WALL OF CHINA

If a wall is a building, then the Great Wall of China is by far the largest building in the world. It is 1,500 miles long—equivalent to the distance between Hamburg and Palermo—and extends from the coast of the Yellow Sea to the steppes of central Asia, from Su-chou in Kansu to Shan-hai-kuan on the Gulf of the Liaotung. In general, it is about 50 feet high, 26 feet wide at the base narrowing to a width of 16 feet at the top, and twice crosses the Huang Ho (Yellow River). In Hopeh it splits into two arms to protect Peking. There must once have been a watchtower every hundred yards or so—making a total of over 40,000. It has been calculated that the Great Wall was constructed from almost 400,000,000 cubic yards of material—enough to build about 120 pyramids of Cheops or to

these border fortifications probably consisted of nothing more th banks of earth with watchtowers.

The Emperor Shih Huang Ti (221–210 BC) was responsible having the first banks constructed for protection against outside In part, he kept to the existing fortifications; for the rest he had ne mounds built in order to deter incursions into his realm.

At this stage there was still no question of one continuous wa Key points on the lines of defence were the towers which had ou walls consisting of enormous bricks (18 by 18 inches). The spa between the outer walls was filled with a mixture of clay, gra and tamarisk branches stamped into place. The towers were abc 30 feet high and 20 feet wide. As yet, walls had not been co

lay a 6-foot-high wall round the equator.

The history of this wall of blood and tears goes back 2,600 years in time, though, contrary to a widely held opinion, the present Great Wall is notably younger. The major part of the present wall dates back to the fifteenth century when China was ruled by the Ming Dynasty. The earliest Chinese walls were not built for defence against foreign enemies but were the result of China's internal affairs. Thus, at the beginning of the sixth century BC, the state of Ch'u protected itself against attacks from the neighbouring states to the north by building a wall along the border. This example was subsequently followed by the states of Ch'i and Wei, and in the fourth century BC by several other neighbouring peoples. In most cases

structed on the clay dyke that ran between the towers, but 1 compressed loess proved so sturdy that to this day parts of the dy have remained intact.

The towers were occupied by sentries. Whenever the mount hordes of the Hun approached, the nearest garrison to the bor fortifications, stationed in a camp or fortress, was alerted. Dur the day flag-like canvasses or smoke signals were used to re the news; at night wire baskets filled with burning torches serv the same purpose. With the aid of poles these baskets were mov up and down to a prearranged rhythm. One of the sentries' du was to keep a broad strip of sand on the approaches to the fortificatic clean and smooth at all times so that the slightest trace of a hos

150

rusion or the presence of spies would not be missed.

At first, the fortifications were built by Emperor Shih Huang Ti's [arm]y. Tradition has it that the work was undertaken by 300,000 [sol]diers. Their efforts, however, were not sufficient to make the [wo]rk advance at the required rate and so the prisons were opened [and] thieves and murderers were sent to the building site. When even [the]se measures proved inadequate a large proportion of the popu[lat]ion was conscripted: according to contemporary reports, every [thi]rd male Chinese was ordered to assist with the building of the [wa]ll. Hundreds of thousands of labourers died of exhaustion, over[wo]rk or starvation. A Chinese lament says: 'If a daughter is born to [yo]u, drown her. If a son is born to you, do not bring him up. Do

In the Chinese annals of the following centuries the talk is no longer of the Great Wall. It was not until the fifth and sixth centuries AD that sparse records about the construction of new barriers began to appear. Marco Polo, who toured the length and breadth of China during the thirteenth century, made no mention of wall-like fortifications along the border. Yet if in those days there were still any substantial remains of Shih Huang Ti's wall, it seems unlikely that they would have escaped his notice.

The plan for a new, more substantial 'wall of 10,000 miles' (the 'mile' works out at 1,079 feet) appears to have emerged in the fourteenth century. The Moguls under Ghenghis Khan and his successors had subjugated China and continued in power for ninety

[not] see now the Great Wall is being built on piles of corpses?' [Bu]t like earlier and later walls, Shih Huang Ti's was only effective [a] deterrent against hostile invasions when adequately guarded [by] soldiers. Undefended the fortification was useless. When, [dur]ing a rebellion in the year 209 BC, soldiers and conscripted [labo]urers left the border area, the Huns within a short time succeeded [in] conquering the areas protected by the Great Wall. While its [out]line remained unfinished, the border wall was useless, and during [the] centuries that followed the Huns broke into China time and [aga]in. Chinese counter-measures were ineffectual, nor were the [trib]utes paid to the Huns or the marriage of their leaders to imperial [prin]cesses of any avail.

years. In the year 1368 the Chinese rebels under the leadership of the peasant's son and novice monk, Chu Yüan-chang (as the Emperor Hung Wu he founded the Ming Dynasty) at last succeeded in driving out the aliens. During the centuries that followed there were constant encroachments by the Mongols. On one occasion

Above: Great Wall of China with watchtower in the mountains of Pa-ta-ling. Left-hand page: the wall follows the steepest mountain contours (left), winds through desolate mountain countryside (above right) and skirts the edge of mountain ranges (below right) to the west of the capital, Peking.

they even took the emperor prisoner. Something had to be done to protect the empire against the attacks from the north. Under the orders of various emperors of the Ming Dynasty, which lasted until 1644, a new edition of the Great Wall was built. In the records of the contemporary Chinese court it was still only entered under the heading 'antiquities'.

In building the Ming wall broad foundations of heavy square stones were laid, on which two strong walls of fired brick were constructed. True to the building methods of Shih Huang Ti, the space between the two walls was filled with a compressed mixture of clay, crushed stone, gravel and bits of brick. A layer of brick the width of a roadway covered the filling. When the two parap were built one on each side, special care was taken to find the m suitable angle for firing crossbows. Rectangular towers were c structed at regular intervals along the wall.

The wall took no heed of obstacles in the terrain. At one en extended well into the Yellow Sea. Ships filled with iron and gra were sunk near the shore and used as a foundation for the w 'The wall extends over mountain ridges to east and west into endless distance, over the steepest heights, down into the deep valleys, sometimes disappearing into the clouds which veil mountain peaks.' (Hesse-Wartegg).

dam Brand, a German merchant who travelled to China from scow in 1692, wrote a graphic account of the walls manned by rds: 'Above, on the wall, there was a watchtower occupied by ut 40 to 50 soldiers upon which an idol's temple was built, which the pennants and flags of the idol and king flew; as we e told, continuous watch should have been held in the afore-tioned watchtower; equally, there was also a watchtower ond the last gate occupied by 20 people . . . Where necessary, wall also had entrances in suitable places which were made y for trading and partly for sorties against the Tartars. Inside outside the wall lay strong fortifications.' As well as the Great

Wall, there are other monumental buildings which also preserve the memory of the Ming Dynasty. Most of the Ming emperors were buried in a vast temple area not far from Peking. Anyone who sets out to see the Great Wall should also pay a visit to the Ming tombs which are approached along an avenue over half a mile long and lined with strange, gigantic sculptures of animals and warriors.

Above: curious sculptures of animals border the so-called Ming Avenue which leads to the tombs of the Ming emperors near Peking. Left-hand page, top to bottom: Ming burial place; warrior figure; animal sculpture near Peking.

153

Temple of unnumbered Buddhas
BOROBUDUR

The Temple of Borobudur not far from Jogjakarta on the island of Java has been called a mountain of the gods—an apt description for the vast religious building for it really is not a single, free-standing structure but a mountain, or at least a hill, which has been covered with blocks of stone. When this, the largest temple in Asia, was built in honour of Buddha during the eighth century AD, Buddhism was already in a decline on the Indian subcontinent. It had been undermined from within by Hindu influences, and the revival of the religion of the Brahmans put an end to the predominance of Buddhism in India. In others parts the tidal-wave of Islam overwhelmed the Buddhist faith.

It was not until about this time that the islands of the Malay archipelago first adopted Buddhism. Hundreds of temples dedicated to Buddha appeared—in central Java alone there were 150. Most of them have long been overgrown by the tropical forest, and this was the fate of the mountain of gods at Borobudur. Not until the nineteenth century was it discovered and the task of excavation begun. A traveller visiting Java at the turn of the century remarked: 'Now that Borobudur has been disentangled from all the debris and the mass of tropical vegetation, one can see that it was a magnificent achievement on the part of some unknown people.'

The dome-shaped building rises to a height of 115 feet in five square terraces surmounted by three flights of steps. A sixth terrace, 364 feet along each side, was subsequently added at the base of the building, presumably because the upper layers of stone threatened to slide away from the sand and clay mixture of the hill, which hardly constituted a suitable foundation. Four flights of stairs lead to the summit of the temple hill. At first glance the overall appearance of the building is confusing because of the countless friezes, niches and domes. To the casual onlooker the truncated pyramid of Borobudur gives the impression of a heavy concertinaed mass. 'It looks like a pie, meticulously made but badly risen,' observed the French art historian Foucher after his first visit to Borobudur.

Foucher was also critical of the fact that from the foot of the stone pyramid it was impossible to see the uppermost platform and, conversely, that the lowest terrace could not be seen from the top. This Foucher ascribed to a mistake on the part of the architect. Were the designers of Borobudur really guilty of bad workmanship? This supposition was accepted for a long time. Architecturally, the building is to be regarded as a stupa. The stupa, which evolved from the rounded shape of burial mounds, can be either a hollow building used to house relics or purely a place of worship without rooms. Most of them consist of a hemispherical, bell-shaped or cylindrical building on a rectangular terrace. Now the designers of Borobudur deviated considerably from the earlier stupa forms, and it was quite some time before it was realized that here was a form of stupa, built in the late Buddhist era, which had been carefully thought out and executed to the last refinement. From this conclusion it did not take long to recognize that the temple's fore-shortened perspective, of which Foucher complained, was no error but was designed for a good reason

The explanation lay in the Buddhist teachings. The building was quite intentionally designed in this way so that from the foot of the shrine the pilgrim could see nothing of the heights to which his religion promised to lead him. The five terraces were clearly intended to symbolize the five stages which had to be covered on the way to inner peace and tranquility—the renunciation of worldly desires, of malevolence and malicious joy, of indolence and doubt. Once the pilgrim arrived at the highest terrace the intermediary stages of conflict were no longer visible from the point of attainment. Accordingly, the highest platform with the summit of the temple symbolized Nirvana, the perfect peace of the soul, the release from the endless circling of the wandering soul, a 'state of absolute independence from the world, which is described by those who have attained it as

Seventy-two bell-shaped domes, known as 'dagobas', crowned the highest circular terrace of Borobudur. Each one contained a statue of Buddha.

155

indescribable heavenly bliss, as salvation'. (H. J. Schoeps). The effort expended in building the temple must even overshadow that put into the pyramids of Egypt. Admittedly, considerably more material was used in building, for example, the Pyramid of Cheops, but the unknown builders of Borobudur took far more trouble over the artistic appearance of their temple. The terrace walls are decorated with 1,400 stone carvings, which altogether add up to a relief three miles long.

Niches with statues of Buddha (of which there are 432) are interjected into this history of Buddhism carved out of stone. The statues which await the pilgrim on the highest circular terrace are hidden under *dagobas*, cloche-like structures of latticed stone, which allow a view into the interior. There are 72 of these 'bells' arranged in three circles around the central tower of the temple, which also contains a statue of Buddha. In beauty and balance this

sculpture is no match for the other figures: a roughly carved sits on a shapeless body. It was assumed that this statue symbo the Buddhist Nirvana, but the explanation is possibly simpler principal statue of Buddha was never finished. Borobudur back into the primeval forest before it could be completed. A my surrounds the 'temple of the countless Buddhas' (that is the t lation of Borobudur). It is thought that the enormous temple used as a place of worship for no more than a few decades. A the year AD 900 society in central Java came to a sudden There is no evidence to suggest that there was a severe na catastrophe or devastating epidemic at this time. A much-disp theory suggests that the inhabitants of central Java fled rather sacrifice all their time and strength to building the temple. 'Perh year after year, insane kings forced the peasants to fetch, stack and build up the enormous blocks,' says A. E. Johann i

on Indonesia. 'Compared with the honour of the gods, the
ur of the royal line, what did the life and health of poor peasants
er . . . ? Anyone with courage took his wife and children and
to the east where new kingdoms were being formed.'
There is much in favour of this theory, especially when one
mbers the nature of the country. It would not be possible to
across the deserts of Egypt without being detected—and the
ces of survival there would in any case be slight. South-east
with its dense forests and abundance of natural food, would
been a different matter—and who would endure a miserable
uffering the lunatic fancies of an absolute monarch when they
d live elsewhere? Absolute power is not only corrupting, it is
self-defeating.

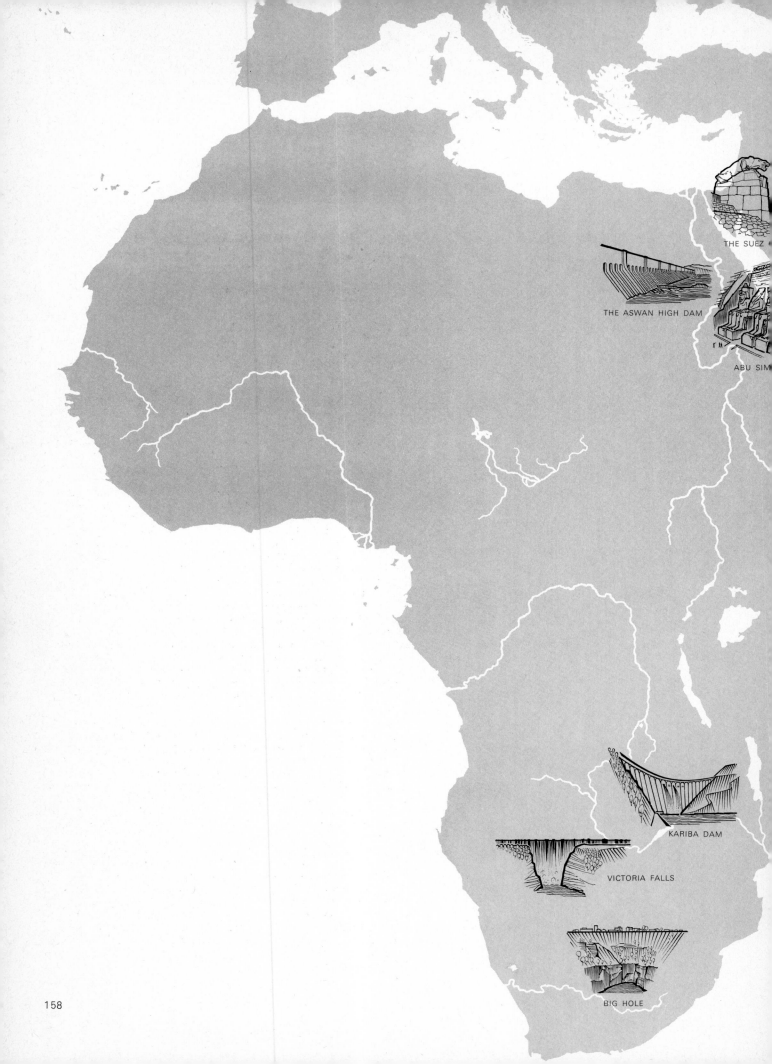

THE SUEZ

THE ASWAN HIGH DAM

ABU SIM

KARIBA DAM

VICTORIA FALLS

BIG HOLE

WONDERS OF AFRICA

On the soil of northern Africa stand the pyramids of Gizeh, the only one of the seven wonders of the ancient world which can still be seen today, and also the oldest buildings in the world to rank amongst its wonders. The sphinx, too, was once regarded as a work of this class.

Most of the other achievements dating back to the time of the pharaohs, such as the step-pyramid at Sakkara or the temple at El Karnak, the buildings of Luxor or the gigantic temple of Hatshepsut near Thebes, pale in comparison with the pyramids. However, there is, in fact, more than just one of the wonders of the world in Egypt. It says in one of the brochures published by the Egyptian information bureau: 'We possess two saleable items in legendary profusion, and they are sunshine and history. The country can boast twelve full months of sunshine and a 5,000-year-old history, including the last remaining wonder of the ancient world.' Tourism is Egypt's third largest and fastest growing industry.

Not so easily accessible are the natural, cultural and technological wonders of black Africa, south of the Sahara. Two of them lie not far apart: namely, the Victoria Falls on the Zambezi, higher and more spectacular than the Niagara Falls in North America, and the Kariba Dam, also on the Zambezi, Africa's largest dam and, after the new Aswan High Dam the dam with the second largest reservoir in the world.

What other wonders has Africa to offer? The rock paintings and engravings in Tanzania, the Sahara and elsewhere should not go unmentioned. Dating back to the New Stone Age and only recently discovered, they are evidence of a time when today's desert area 'cursed by the gods' must once have been a fertile land. The remains of Zimbabwe in Rhodesia mystified archaeologists for some time, but it is now known that the area lying to the north of the Limpopo was the centre of an African civilization long before the beginning of white colonization, and that the oldest walls of Zimbabwe were built during the European Middle Ages.

Among the wonders of Africa one could also include the national parks and game reserves, such as the famous Kruger National Park in South Africa, the Tsavo National Park in Kenya, the Serengeti Plains and the Ngorongoro Crater in Tanzania. In these protected areas it is possible to see lions and elephants, gnus and gazelles, zebras and antelopes—the whole animal kingdom of Africa in its natural habitat. In East Africa particularly, countless 'bungalow-villages' for tourists have sprung up. Here, too, rises the highest mountain in Africa, Kilimanjaro, around whose snow-capped peak hover the clouds.

159

The first canal to connect the Mediterranean with the Red Sea was built at the time of the pharaohs. The Persian kings and later the Ptolemies had the waterway renovated, but during the ninth century, under the rule of the Arabs, the canal silted up. Napoleon was the first person to have a new scheme worked out, but owing to a miscalculation it was never put into practice. It was thought necessary to build a canal with large locks because the level of the Red Sea was 30 feet higher than that of the Mediterranean Sea. In fact, the difference was no more than 30 inches.

England breathed a sigh of relief. A Suez Canal under French control could have threatened British predominance in India. And so, when in 1847 the canal scheme was taken up again, every possible effort was made by the British to prevent its realization. In the long run, however, their strategies failed, and in 1854 a

possession of Egypt and the Canal Zone. When in 1956 the Egypt proclaimed the nationalization of the canal, the consequence the Suez crisis of 1956, in which Britain and France combined Israel to attack Egypt. Intervention by the UN brought an en hostilities, but the canal remained the centre of conflict in the East and has remained closed since the Arab-Israeli war of 196

The canal, measuring 100 miles long, is up to 42 feet deep 195 to 330 feet wide on the bottom (as a result of several extensic It has long been one of the most sensitive nerves of internati traffic. In the 1950s an average of 72 ships a day travelled thro it, making it the busiest seaway for heavy-tonnage shipping in world. Two of every three of the ships which passed through canal carried crude oil. The passage for a freighter normally about £6,250, but this expense was worth the reduction in mile

concession agreement was signed between the Egyptian Khedive Said Pasha and the Frenchman Ferdinand de Lesseps. Five years later work began on the plans for the canal which had been drawn up by an Austrian, Alois Negrelli, and on 17 November 1869 the canal was ceremonially opened with oriental splendour.

The original estimated cost of 200,000,000 francs proved to be an underestimate. In fact, the actual costs must have amounted to double that figure. Initially, Egypt and France had each owned half the Suez Canal Company shares. But the coffers of the Egyptian Khedive were empty and in 1875 Ismail, Said Pasha's successor, sold his share to the British. Seven years later the British took

On, say, the journey from London to Bombay, travelling through Suez Canal instead of around the Cape of Good Hope, red the length of the journey by forty per cent.

Above: a freighter travelling from the Bitter Lake into the north reaches. Right-hand page: the statue of Vicomte de Lesseps (uｐ left) was knocked down by the Egyptians after the expropriatio the canal. Above right: excavation work during the building of canal. Centre right: the 'Aigle', the first ship to travel through canal. Below right: passing into Timsah Lake. Pages 160–161: exit from the canal into the Red Sea.

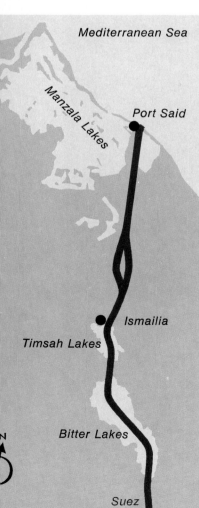

Mediterranean Sea

Manzala Lakes

Port Said

Ismailia

Timsah Lakes

Bitter Lakes

Suez

Gulf of Suez

Moving the pharaoh

ABU SIMBEL

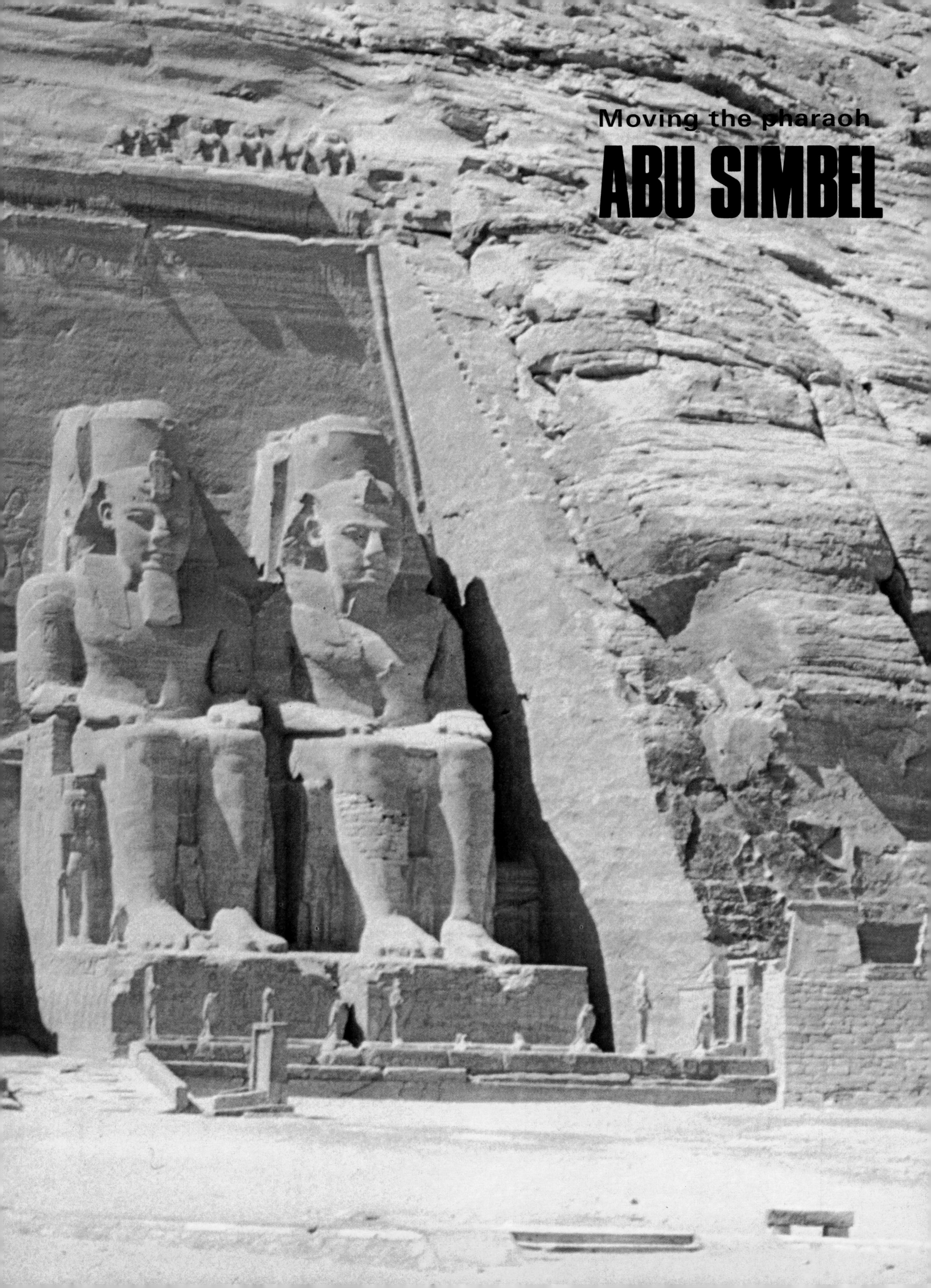

'We lay in an awkward position so that we had to climb up the slope on all fours,' the art historian Julius Meier-Graefe reported, 'and then we stood in front of four giants, feeling at first somewhat uneasy in their strange company. Including their crowns they must have been a good sixty-five feet high, and, as their feet rested on pedestals, we hardly reached as high as their ankles. There they sit quite peacefully in pairs on either side of the entrance, whose surround is no higher than their knees. Like everything else there, they are carved out of the grey stone of the mountain.'

This description of the colossal sculptures and buildings on the west bank of the Nile between the first and second cataracts could not come from anyone visiting Egypt today, for the temples which were carved out of rock over 3,200 years ago have taken to wandering. They are fleeing the Nile whose waters, dammed up to form the 370-mile-long Lake Nasser, are flooding further portions of the river valley.

Both temples of Abu Simbel (near the large temple, with its colossal statues measuring over sixty-five feet high, there is a second, smaller one) were built at the command of Rameses II (1290–1224 BC), also known as the Great. He himself did everything to preserve his memory for posterity in a mass of enormous buildings. Of all the pharaohs he probably left behind the largest number of buildings and sculptures, in which he was always the prominent figure in the foreground. According to the critic Egon Friedell, 'His works reveal a disagreeable desire for the swaggering effects of size and a coarse self-glorification. Whole forests of stone giants recall his features *ad nauseam.*'

Without doubt the rock temples of Abu Simbel are the most enormous creations of the publicity-conscious king. The fact that these creations have been called 'as grandiose as they are pointless' (Friedell) detracts neither from their splendour, nor the skill with which they were made, nor their historical value. In front of the temple the seated figure of the pharaoh reigns in a multiplicity of duplicates. The same figure is repeated eight times inside the mountain where the halls and walls, penetrating 65 yards into the side of the mountain, are decorated with splendid wall paintings and reliefs. Three enormous 30-foot-high statues of the pharaoh and his wife Nefertari decorate the façade of the smaller temple. Once it had been established that the Nile dam would flood both the temples (in the same way as the reservoir of the old Aswan Dam had covered the famous Philae Island), UNESCO turned to all civilized nations with a cry for help—'The gods are drowning!'.

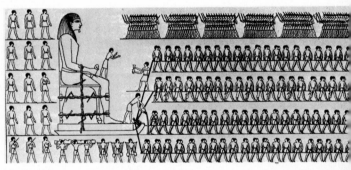

Help came from many places. After the first plan to protect Abu Simbel with a dam had been discarded and the idea of putting the temples on an enormous platform of reinforced concrete which could then be raised had proved impracticable, the proposal of a German firm was finally accepted. This involved cutting the statues and chambers piece by piece out of the rock, transporting the fragments to a high safe place and then reassembling everything on the new site. The waters of the Nile may rise over Abu Simbel but the Pharaohs are safe in their new home.

Above: ancient Egyptian festival at the Temple of Abu Simbel (drawing from the year 1886). Centre: transporting a colossal statue in ancient Egypt. Below: the gold mask of Tutankhamun was found in 1922. A pharaoh of the previous dynasty (the Eighteenth) he died at the age of eighteen. His features are no doubt as much idealised in this superb funerary mask as those of Rameses II at Abu Simbel. But the style of portraiture is strikingly different, and the boy pharaoh left no monuments.

Right-hand page: façade of the smaller temple with statues of Rameses and Nefertari (above); the statues of the large temple, having been taken apart, are carefully put together again on the new site.

Pages 164–165: the large temple on its former site.

gypt's livelihood depends on a single river, the ·Nile. For centuries agricultural land in this, the land of the Pharaohs, has been confined to a narrow strip on each side of the river. It was seventy-five years ago that the first sizeable dam was constructed near Aswan, about 600 miles from the Mediterranean Sea. Following several extensions, it now has a capacity of 320,000,000,000 cubic feet of water, used principally for irrigation.

The new scheme provides a dam 330 feet high and over two miles long with a reservoir, called Lake Nasser, extending 300 miles and holding 5,500,000 million cubic feet of water. Backed by finance from Suez Canal revenue and Russian loans, the project has been under construction since 1960. As many as 30,000 workmen at one time have been engaged on the site, assisted by technologists (2,000 engineers alone) and machinery from the Soviet Union. Tens of thousands of Nubians and Sudanese are being resettled. The new dam should increase the country's farm land by 30 per cent (about 320,000 acres). The power station built into the dam is the largest in the world and will produce ten milliard kilowatt-hours annually—ten times more than current sources provide. No wonder that the Egyptians look with hope at the desert building site of Sadd el Aali

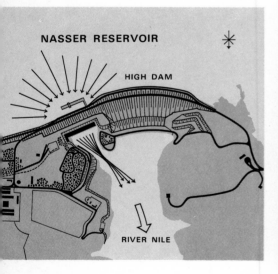

NASSER RESERVOIR

HIGH DAM

RIVER NILE

which, with an area of almost six square miles, is the largest building site in the world. The mighty river, the source of Egypt's life for thousands of years, is being harnessed to the needs of man. The ancient annual bounty of floodwater is no longer sufficient for the country's needs.

Amid enormous earthworks and reinforced concrete the new High Dam rises. Above: sketch of the final layout.

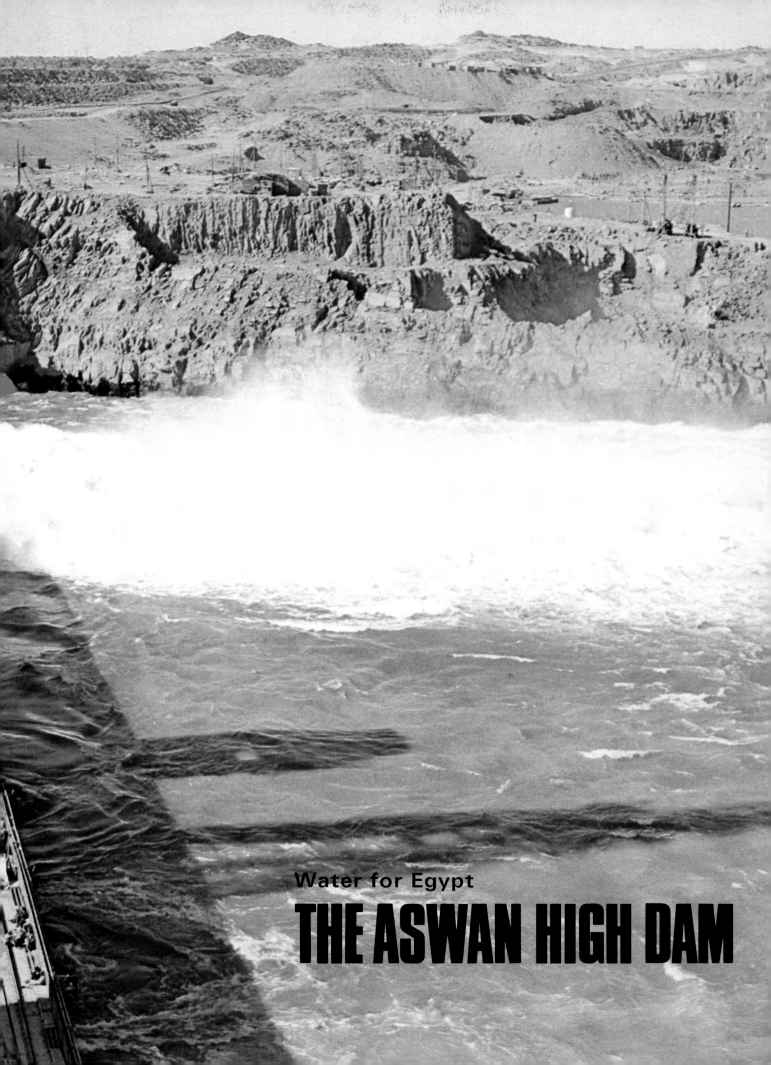

Water for Egypt

THE ASWAN HIGH DAM

the thundering waters of the Zambezi

VICTORIA FALLS

A E. Johann, a traveller well acquainted with the African
continent, once described the Victoria Falls on the Zambezi
as 'Africa's greatest wonder'. On more than one occasion he
has stood at the top of the 400-foot ravine into which the
Zambezi, at this point over a mile wide, pours at a rate of up
to 140,000,000 cubic feet per minute. On one recent tour of Africa,
Johann made a detour of over 600 miles just to see the falls again.

Johann described this encounter: 'Out of the white night the
deep roaring of the Victoria Falls welled up against me, thick and
heavy. I stood and stared, and my heart beat faster—a gust of wind
had blown away the thick wall of spray: now a rainbow arched high

over the edge which shimmered in the moonlight as the w
crashed over it into the depths below.'

The first white man to visit and describe the Victoria Falls was
Scots missionary Dr David Livingstone (1813–73), who journe
to the falls in a fragile canoe. Dozens of miles away he could alre
see the 'five fingers', five misty columns rising from the main
of the Zambezi which are separated from each other by s
islands. Livingstone recklessly steered towards one of the isla
right on the brink of the precipice. 'We were only a short sto
throw away from the falls but still we could not make out wl
exactly the enormous mass of water disappeared to. It seemed

the ground suddenly swallowed it up, for the opposite edge of the chasm into which the river poured was no more than twenty-five yards away. I could not comprehend what I saw until, with fear in my heart, I crawled to the extreme edge and stunned with amazement looked down into the broad abyss.'

The chasm, whose width Livingstone gave as twenty-five yards, must be at least three times as wide today. Not far from the falls the Cape Cairo Railway Bridge crosses the canyon, and a luxurious hotel makes it easy for globe-trotters to stare in awe at the masses of water plunging with an 'unearthly thundering roar' into the abyss below.

The falls always offer new and exciting perspectives, whether viewed from the Zambezi gorge (above), from the air (left), or through the luxuriant tropical vegetation (far left).

Africa's largest dam
KARIBA DAM

For some years there has been a new lake in southern central Africa on the border between Rhodesia and Zambia. Over 170 miles long, up to 20 miles wide and covering an area of 1,100 square miles, it is a match for any of the old lakes in Africa, and yet it is only a reservoir—the largest in the African continent, however, and the second largest in the world (after the Bratskaya Reservoir on the Angara in the USSR), with a capacity of over 200,000 million cubic yards.

Africa is immeasurably rich in water power. A good third of the water power potential of the whole world lies in Africa, but it is only potential, for barely one per cent of it has been exploited yet. The favourable topographical conditions, however, facilitate further development. Southern central Africa represents an enormous basin from which the great rivers have to make their way through the high mountain ranges. The places where the rivers break through the mountains are ideal for building dams.

The Zambezi flows through such a breach, the Kariba Gorge, about 125 miles downstream from the Victoria Falls. When, after 1955, this gorge was blocked off by a 430-foot-high dam wall, the river dammed up behind it to form the great lake. A power station converts the force of the water into electricity. Built at a cost of £125,000,000 it went into operation in 1960. It is designed to produce 8,000,000,000 kilowatt-hours for the rapidly expanding industries of Rhodesia and Zambia.

At first, the inhabitants of the Zambezi Valley viewed the building operations with distrust. They did not believe the engineers who told them that their houses would soon be standing under dozens of feet of water. Over 25,000 Batonga (and vast numbers of wild animals had to be evacuated before the water began to rise. The Kariba Dam has changed the appearance of the country.

Beginning in 1955 the Kariba Dam (above) was constructed 125 miles downstream from the Victoria Falls. Enormous jets of water spurt through the open sluices from the lake (below). Right-hand page: the largest dam in Africa has bottled up the Zambezi to form a huge lake.

Pages 174–175: the stupendous dam and the newly formed lake behind it. The rescue of great numbers of animals from the rising waters was a much-praised undertaking – Africa's wild life has need of every aid in preservation. But new problems have arisen with the loss of so much land; ecologists are studying the disappearance of certain species of fish – and the arrival of great quantities of eels – with great concern.

In the middle of the South African city of Kimberley an enormous chasm, deceptively like a natural volcanic crater, sinks into the ground. The upper part, almost a mile in circumference, is shaped like a gigantic funnel, while lower down the sides drop vertically to a depth of over 3,600 feet. The bottom cannot be seen: water has seeped in, filling the hole to half its depth.

This cavity, known as Big Hole, is one of South Africa's major tourist attractions. It was dug by human hand over a period of forty-three years, and to it Kimberley owes its existence. Even though Big Hole lies in the middle of the city, it will never be filled in because the inhabitants of Kimberley regard it as a sort of inverted monument commemorating the Great Diamond Rush. Where there is now a hole, there was once a hill called Colesberg Kopje. Here on 16 July 1871 a gang of diamond prospectors sought their fortune. Fleetwood Rawstorne and his friends, known as the 'Red Cap Union' after their red head-gear, had already tried in many other places but had never yet stumbled on a find of any significance. On Colesberg Kopje they struck lucky at the first attempt, finding many small but unblemished diamonds near the surface. The very same night they staked their claims. By the next morning dozens of other prospectors, also anxious to secure

mining rights, had arrived at the site, and barely a year later there were over 50,000 digging round the spot which had once been a hill.

Over the years more than 14,000,000 carats of diamonds were found in Big Hole. In order to extract them 25,000,000 tons of earth and rock had to be brought up. The rubble was deposited in a wide circle round Big Hole and formed the foundations of the town of Kimberley. Since 1914 Big Hole has no longer been worked. Although there is no doubt that its depths still hold vast quantities of diamonds, it would not be profitable to mine them. Moreover the age of the independent prospectors has passed. The government ceased to issue licences a long time ago, and the few remaining diamond prospectors in Kimberley confine themselves to searching through the rubble thrown up by road works or by the demolition of an old house, but the yield is very small.

On a visit to Big Hole Lord Randolph Churchill, father of Winston Churchill, is reported to have observed rather wistfully 'And all that just for the vanity of women!' To which a woman in his party smartly retorted, 'But also for the wickedness of men!'

The deepest excavation
BIG HOLE

Big Hole, the biggest man-made hole, looks like an enormous volcanic crater (centre). Only a few of the old prospectors who once dug here for diamonds now remain (far left). Today diamond mining is highly industrialized. Above: sorting rough diamonds.

179

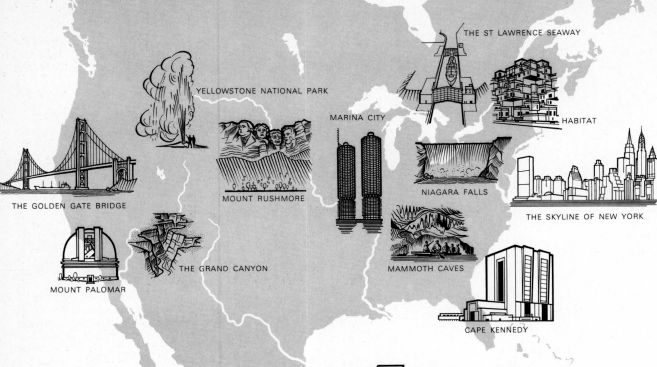

THE ST LAWRENCE SEAWAY

YELLOWSTONE NATIONAL PARK

MARINA CITY

HABITAT

THE GOLDEN GATE BRIDGE

MOUNT RUSHMORE

NIAGARA FALLS

THE SKYLINE OF NEW YORK

MOUNT PALOMAR

THE GRAND CANYON

MAMMOTH CAVES

CAPE KENNEDY

CHICHEN ITZA

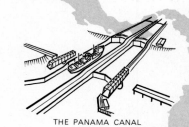

THE PANAMA CANAL

MACHU PICCHU

WONDERS OF AMERICA

BRASILIA

RIO DE JANEIRO

IGUAÇU FALLS

No continent in the world is so richly blessed with natural and man-made wonders as America, and in this respect none can compare with the sheer variety of extraordinary sights in North and South America. It would be difficult to think of a single category in which North or South America cannot supply the superlative example. The most beautiful city in the world? According to general opinion, Rio de Janeiro. The largest observatory? Without question the observatory on Mount Palomar. The longest and deepest gorge? By a long way the Grand Canyon of the Colorado River. The most famous suspension bridge in the world? The Golden Gate Bridge in San Francisco. The city with the most daring modern design? Brasilia. The largest rocket launching site? Cape Kennedy. The list is endless. But obviously not everything that is the biggest, the highest or the longest in the world is necessarily also one of the wonders of the world, although there is a strong connection between this concept and superlative achievement. If, however, one applies other standards, such as beauty, originality or ingenuity, one would find such a profusion of remarkable and wonderful sights that it would be difficult to arrive at a just selection.

Canada, represented here by the St Lawrence Seaway, the Niagara Falls (half of which are in the USA) and the Habitat living complex in Montreal (described by some as epoch-making, by others as worthless) could also, perhaps, contribute the Trans-Canada Highway or one of its huge dams to this collection. From the United States it would be easy to gather a good dozen natural, cultural or technological marvels of above-average interest—one need only think of the Sequoia National Park, the Capitol in Washington, Death Valley, the Tennessee Valley or the fine highway that runs along the west coast.

And South America? The ruins dating back to pre-Colombian times are so numerous that the chief examples alone would fill a whole book: Copan and Uxmal, Tikal and Piedras Negras of the Maya; Tehuantepec and Tenochtitlan (now Mexico City), Teotihuacan and Tula built by the ancient peoples of Central America, Tiahuanaco and Cuzco, Tomebamba and Pisac founded by the Incas and their forebears—it is impossible to count the number of temple ruins, let alone relate the history of every building, how it was built and by whom, when and how it was discovered, and all the details that give it special interest.

The mighty Andes, the pampas of Argentina, the barren plateaus and cold deserts of the south, great construction projects like the Maracaibo bridge in Venezuela, the strange world of the Brazilian forests, the Amazon itself—largest river in the world—all these might well be included; but the resulting book would be enormous—and might prove too heavy to lift!

ips' highway in the heart of America

HE ST LAWRENCE
SEAWAY

The five Great Lakes in the borderland between the USA and Canada could more fittingly be called a sea. Sometimes they actually are referred to as the Mediterranean of North America, for the combined area of Lakes Superior, Huron, Michigan, Erie and Ontario is roughly equal to the area of the whole of West Germany. The outlet for the Great Lakes is the St Lawrence which flows into the Atlantic. It was along this river that European discoverers, Jacques Cartier is perhaps the most famous of them, first penetrated to the heart of North America.

The plan to develop the 2,300-mile-long reach of water between the mouth of the St Lawrence and the city of Duluth on Lake Superior into a gigantic waterway is already history. The Canadians were particularly in favour of the scheme; the Americans showed less enthusiasm. But in 1932 the two countries signed an agreement for the joint development of the St Lawrence Seaway. The technical difficulties—different levels between the lakes, rapids in the St Lawrence, the need to build large locks and canals—had to be coped with, as well as the question of financing the project. It took decades before some US companies overcame their reservations and agreed to take part in the great investment.

By 1959 the largest inland waterway in the world was complete. Ocean-going

freighters can now travel from the Atlantic into the heart of North America. In the course of the voyage they are raised to a height of 600 feet above sea level by a series of sixteen locks.

Countless new locks (left: Eisenhower Lock; above: lock near Montreal) made the St Lawrence Seaway into the largest inland waterway in the world.

183

The mighty waters
NIAGARA FALLS

The Niagara is one of the shortest rivers in the world. Its course from Lake Erie to Lake Ontario is only 25 miles, but over this short distance the river has to negotiate a 350-foot drop in level. This it achieves partly by the steep slope of its course and partly by a waterfall of gigantic proportions, the Niagara Falls, which lie in the Great Lakes area on the borderland between the USA and Canada. The American fall is 984 feet wide and 200 feet deep; the Canadian fall, on the other hand, is about three times as wide and 207 feet deep. About 555,000 cubic yards of water per minute plunge over the edge. White men first heard details about the falls from the Indians who believed that the water demons required the lives of two people every year. In 1657 the natural wonder was recorded on a French map, but it was not until twenty years later that the first white explorers, the French traveller La Salle and his Belgian companion Louis Hennepin, a monk, penetrated as far as the falls. The first reports recorded some incredible 'facts'—in one it is said that the water plunged 650 feet into the gorge, another maintained that the thundering of the falls could be heard for miles.

How were the Niagara Falls formed? During the last Ice Age North America was covered by an enormous glacier. On the southern edge of this ice mass the melted waters formed an inland sea which at first flowed into the Gulf of Mexico and later into the Atlantic. For reasons not yet fully understood the Great Lakes were left as the remnants of this Ice Age sea. A ridge of land separated the lower-lying Lake Ontario from the other lakes, which now lack outlets. Under the pressure of the water, Lake Erie developed an overflow into Lake Ontario, and in the course of time the precipitant masses of water wore away the slate and limestone of the ridge. Had the precipice originally been really close to Lake Ontario, then it would have gradually receded farther and farther through the effects of erosion, leaving behind a channel through which the water would have flowed to Lake Ontario.

This is what is now happening. Near Lake Erie, where it is almost 4,000 feet wide, the Niagara flows relatively smoothly. Some miles downstream from the lake, it divides into two channels which enclose an elongated island. Four miles above the falls the two arms reunite. The separation into the smaller American and larger Canadian falls does not begin until immediately above the precipice, where Goat Island rises from the bed of the enormous river, taking up almost a quarter

Panorama of the Niagara Falls, showing the smaller American fall (left) and larger Canadian fall, the Horseshoe Fall (right).

of its width—at this point some 4,900 feet.

A traveller once described the experience: 'Disconcerted, the human being stands in front of the green wall as it swirls down.' Once over the precipice the masses of water, however, soon calm down again. Close to the foot of the falls chugs a small steamer, the *Maid of the Mist*, which offers an impressive view of the thundering, spraying, steaming water. Even the critical Karl Baedeker gave this experience a two-star rating. Day and night the masses of water gnaw at the rim of the precipice, eating it away at the rate of one yard every year, and some thousands of years from now the falls will reach Lake Erie. The masses of rock precipitated into the gorge below are creating a problem for the experts who fear that the American falls, in particular, could decline into boring rapids unless somebody hits on a good idea for clearing away the rubble which in some places already reaches half-way up the precipice.

In winter the falls make a fantastic picture. Below the falls the Niagara freezes over thickly where the water strikes the ground. Ice floes plunge over the edge from above and stack up to form enormous icebergs. Hans Bohrdt, a German traveller, described this scene: 'No fairy castle built of crystal and gems could be more beautiful.'

Engineers observe the phenomenon more soberly: to them it has always been an extravagance not to utilize the thundering water as it plunges downward 200 feet. During the 1890s the first attempt was made to harness some of this energy, estimated at 50,000,000 horse power; the result was a mere 5,000-horse-power turbine generator.Today the waterfalls are already producing about 3,000,000 horse power. On the American side, about $2\frac{1}{2}$ miles upstream from the falls, the river is tapped by a double channel which leads to the industrial estates lying $3\frac{1}{2}$ miles downstream from the falls, where thirteen generators with an output of 150,000 kilowatts operate. Although the water is taken from the falls mainly at night and during the winter months, the generation of power causes a considerable fluctuation in the water level of the River Niagara, the variation sometimes amounting to about 30 feet.

Not that this worries the tourists. Since the USA, like Canada, built observation towers near the falls—at the moment there are some as high as 450 feet—a comfortable bird's-eye view, rather than a dangerous post on the bank, has become the preferred way of watching this natural spectacle.

Top to bottom: Horseshoe Fall; one of the observation towers on the Canadian side of the falls; the American falls in winter; one of the adventurers who descended the falls (and survived the experience), Laussier, a Canadian. He made the trip in a rubber ball in 1928. Left-hand page: view of the Horseshoe and American falls.

Montreal's house-mountain
HABITAT

Will houses one day be produced on a conveyor belt like cars? Moshe Safdie, the twenty-eight-year-old Israeli-born designer of the Habitat living complex, the architectural sensation of the 1967 World Fair at Montreal, is sure they will. He maintains that 'If we were to build our cars in the same way as we build our houses, very few of us would be able to afford one.' According to him there is no practicable solution to the housing problem other than the house-mountain, the pyramid made up of uniform sections which can be assembled in a variety of ways.

The Canadian authorities showed considerable courage when they gave Safdie, scarcely an experienced architect, the chance to realize his pet project. As a basis, Safdie developed a concrete box 40 f long, and 20 feet wide and 10 feet high. Cast on the spot out special concrete, 254 of these 85-ton units were stacked one top of the other to form the pyramid—lofty, surrounded by space first glimpse a bit startling, but on closer inspection thoroug convincing. From the 254 concrete boxes 158 flats of various si were created. In arranging them Safdie's aim was to ensure t each house should receive as much sunlight as possible. The yo architect found the basis for his arrangement in a textbook of bot by the British scholar D'Arcy Wentworth Thompson. The Hab gardens also receive sufficient sunlight. Each dwelling is equip

at least one small garden plot. In addition, this twelve-storey [resid]ential mountain has wide streets (up to 16 feet) traversing the [...] heights, playgrounds, business premises and restaurants. The [...] of the Habitat complex was almost £7,000,000—a lot of [mon]ey for 158 homes. But the stacked concrete boxes of Montreal [are o]nly a beginning. Moshe Safdie is already planning a 1,000-unit [...] mid twenty storeys high, which he has discussed with the [Indi]an government. In the next thirty-five years India will need [...]000,000 homes; Safdie has proposed to build them according [to th]e technique tried out in Montreal.

[In] the meantime, however, arguments about Habitat are still

raging. Opinions vary from outright rejection to the conviction that Habitat will become one of Montreal's main attractions, or that Moshe Safdie is one of the most brilliant architects in the world and can be considered the legitimate heir to Le Corbusier.

Above: concrete boxes boldly stacked one on top of another – Habitat from below. Left-hand-page: the St Lawrence River and the exhibition site (above); living room in one of the Habitat homes (left); 'High Streets' in the lofty heights of the twelve-storey Habitat mountain (right).
Pages 188-189: general view of Habitat with the St Lawrence River.

191

Symbol of the super-city

THE SKYLINE OF NEW YORK

tephen Potter, who knew the American super-city well, once remarked that the skyscrapers of New York are so superhuman in size that they can only be compared with what really is superhuman. They can only be measured against the sky itself. As the traveller approaches from the sea, the troop rises above the horizon like vast inorganic growths. They loom bigger and bigger until at last one is confronted by the mighty specimens of downtown Manhattan.

The skyline of New York, which has grown up during the last six decades, is a collection of office blocks unequalled for size anywhere in the world, in spite of the fact that the techniques of highrise building perfected in America have been adopted in almost every country. The birthplace of the skyscraper, however, is not New York but Chicago, where the Home Insurance Building, de-

signed by Major Le-Baron Jenny, was built as long ago as 1 In New York there were regulations which prohibited the struction of buildings over a certain specified height, and it was until these restrictions were relaxed that really tall, multi-st buildings appeared on Manhattan Island. In 1908 the skyscr for Singers, the sewing machine manufacturers was finis With 47 storeys and a height of 613 feet, it was for a period c months the tallest building in the world. Then it was outstrippe the 50-storey building of a life assurance company, which ra the record to 698 feet.

Even in antiquity tall buildings were a symbol of power strength; the most famous example is the Tower of Babylon, ar Ancient Rome there were twelve-storey houses measuring 115 high. For a long time the 528-foot-high tower of Ulm Mi

esented the limit permitted by building techniques. Any building reciably higher than that would not have been able to support its weight, and the foundations would have been crushed under enormous load of the superstructure. Skyscrapers, therefore, d not be built until men learned the technique of using a frame-k of steel supports on which the walls could simply be hung. d in hand with the discovery of the steel-framed building went development of concrete which soon led to the reinforced crete building. The potential of steel-frame building was fully oited by Gustave Eiffel when he built his famous tower. As far building techniques were concerned, the first American sky-pers were the progeny of the Eiffel Tower.

t the beginning of the First World War there were already ten dings in New York over 700 feet high. During the decade that

followed, the ambition of many large firms was to enrich the skyline of New York with an office block of their own. In 1930 the Chrysler Building was officially opened. With 77 floors and a height of 1,003 feet, it was taller even than the Eiffel Tower. A year later the Empire State Building was completed: 102 storeys, 1,246 feet high (subsequently 1,469 feet, after the addition of the television aerial), 6,400 windows, 67 lifts, office and business premises with an area of over 40 acres, weight 308,000 tons, capacity about 50,000 people. It took 3,500 workmen just over one year to build it. With that, a peak was reached which was not surpassed for nearly forty years.

Skyline of New York. Left to right: UN Building, Empire State Building, Chrysler Building, Pan-Am Building.

Technically, there is no problem in building even taller skyscrapers. But the skyscraper boom of the 1920s led to a surplus of city office space; it took ten years to let all the rooms in the Empire State Building. Skyscrapers that were allowed to shoot up too high proved to be unprofitable. After the Empire State Building everything stayed within more modest limits until the 1960s when the Pan-Am building, largest (but not highest) office block in the world, was built. The majestic RCA building in the Rockefeller Center (70 storeys), the Lincoln Building (53 storeys) and the extensive 554-foot-high building of the United Nations with its 39 storeys, one of the most beautiful buildings in New York.

A modern city needs towers 'as accents, as exclamation marks, so to speak, wrote Wolf Schneider in *Babylon is Everywhere*, his history of the development of the city. 'The New Yorkers have perhaps put a few exclamation marks too many; but where arrogance is paired with such sky-storming boldness it is stunning. And in the end we can regard the towers of New York as a general advertisement for our century, displayed in its liveliest city.'

After its skyline, the second most famous symbol of the city with 15,000,000 inhabitants (including all the suburbs) is the Statue of Liberty at the entrance to New York harbour. It was erected in 1886 on Bedloe's Island (now Liberty Island) as a present from France for the centenary celebrations of the American Declaration of Independence. The 150-foot-high goddess of freedom was designed by the Alsatian sculptor, Frédéric-Auguste Bartholdi after Roman examples.

Gustave Eiffel contributed the money for the steel structure that was to support the giant statue. The steel framework was covered with thick, hammered copper plates which altogether weighed over 100 tons. The cost of producing the statue—about £125,000—was raised by French citizens.

The building of the base, which cost not much less than the statue itself, was the responsibility of the Americans. On Bedloe's Island they constructed a 154-foot-high substructure resembling a pedestal, with 167 steps leading up it. In June 1885 the *Isere* brought the parts for the Statue of Liberty to New York, carefully packed in 214 cases. A year later work started on building the monument. The last rivet was put into place on 28 October 1886, during the opening ceremonies conducted by President Grover Cleveland. On the same day the torch held in the goddess's raised hand was lit for the first time.

The Statue of Liberty was later proclaimed a national monument, and a building for the American immigration museum was erected at the foot of the statue. In 1965 the neighbouring Ellis Island, once the famous immigration centre of the USA, was included in the protected area of the Statue of Liberty National Monument; at a cost of 6,000,000 dollars, the second island was developed as a park and museum.

Empire State Building (above), Rockefeller Center (below). Right-hand page: the Statue of Liberty (below right) is one of the symbols of New York. Above: visitors in the head of the 150-foot-high statue – it holds forty people. Below left: New York in the nineteenth century.

196

MAMMOTH CAVES

In 1809 a hunter wandering near the Green River in the heart of Kentucky found the entrance to a subterranean cave—a chance find that, though he could hardly have suspected it at the time, was to lead to the discovery of the largest cave system in the world. Over the years subterranean passages, chambers and ravines extending for more than 150 miles were discovered on five different levels lying one above the other. Spectacular stalagmites and stalactites, conical limestone and gypsum formations, extensive rivers, a lake, blind fishes and crabs were also found; finally, bones dating back to a time when the caves must have been a refuge for some primeval people, were unearthed from piles of debris. It soon became apparent that the Mammoth Caves were not simply an isolated phenomenon, but belonged to an extensive system which even today has not been fully explored. It is estimated that in this region of Kentucky there are

at least 60,000 caves extending over an area of more than 9,500 square miles. The United States government has made the area into a national park, known as 'Mammoth Caves National Park'.

A journey on the subterranean Echo River: the boat is steered by one of the park rangers (right). Above: the 'Drape Room'.

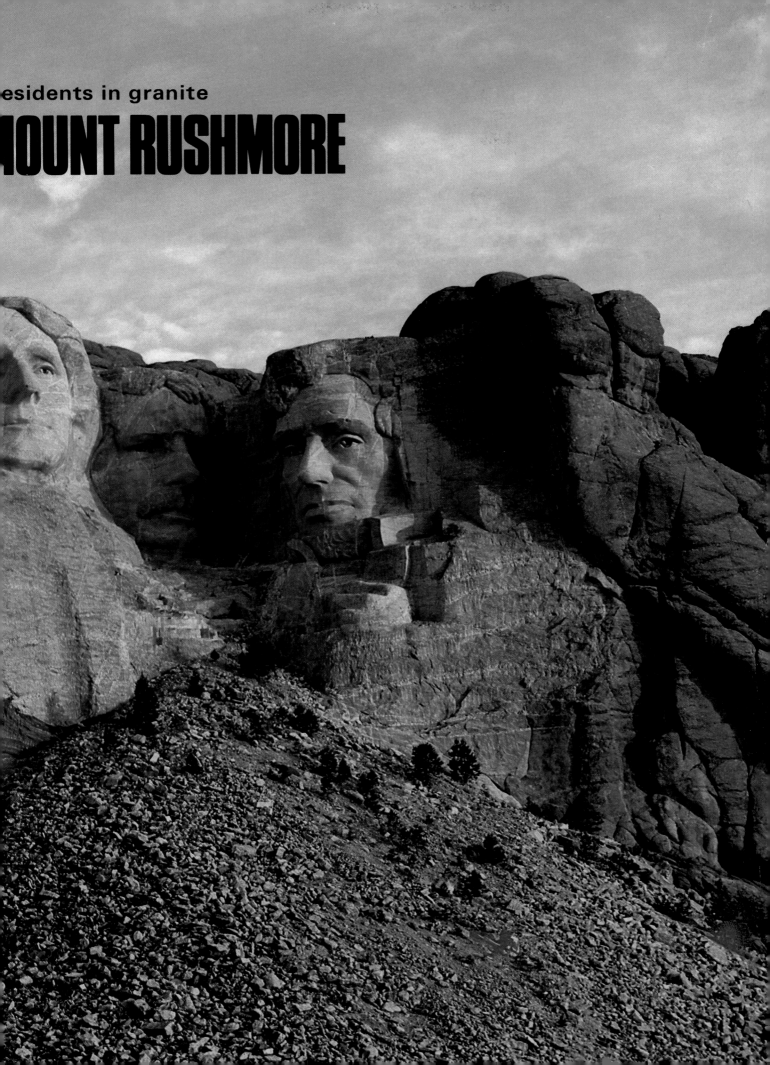

esidents in granite

OUNT RUSHMORE

It took almost fifteen years to build America's largest monument, the gallery of presidents in the Black Hills of South Dakota, where the heads of Washington, Jefferson, Theodore Roosevelt and Lincoln were carved, drilled and blasted out of solid granite. Gutzon Borglum, a well-known painter and sculptor in the United States, hit on the idea of copying the ancient Egyptians who had carved statues and whole temples in the mountains along the Nile. Why could the same thing not be done in the USA? Borglum's choice of site was the 6,673 foot high Mount Rushmore, whose peaks of bare rock tower high above the surrounding country.

At first he had intended to carve only one president's head. It was not possible to foresee at this stage whether the money for further portraits could be raised; moreover, selecting the presidents to be portrayed was a problem.

In 1927 the first scaffold was erected, and an army of workmen began to blast and drill the bust of George Washington (1732–99), the first president. Borglum himself supervised the work, climbing the scaffolding every day to give advice on where to go ahead with caution and where to drive deep into the rock in order to form the 65-foot-high head. Granite dust made life difficult for the workmen; they had to wear protective masks. At the foot of the mountain the rubble which had fallen away grew into an enormous heap.

The second head to appear was that of Thomas Jefferson, the third president of the USA (1743–1826) which, following the natural line of the mountain, lay set back slightly from the Washington portrait. By the time this colossal bust was finished the date was 1936. Half a million tons of granite rubble lay at the foot of the mountain. The gigantic sculptures were already a great tourist attraction, visited in 1936 alone by over 200,000 people. Even the ruling president appeared on the site to judge for himself how the protracted task was progressing.

Theodore Roosevelt (1856–1919), the twenty-sixth president of the USA, was considered worthy of immortalization as the third great American on the summit of Mount Rushmore. Finally, somewhat removed from the first trio, the bust of Abraham Lincoln (1809–65), the sixteenth president of the United States, appeared, but Gutzon Borglum did not live to see its completion. He died in 1941, fourteen years after work on the project had started which his son, Lincoln, completed soon afterwards.

Now over 1,500,000 people a year go to the Black Hills of South Dakota to see the Mount Rushmore Memorial, one of the fifteen national monuments in the USA. The 'Altar of Democracy' has become one of the chief attractions in North America. A particularly large crowd gathers to watch its annual overhaul. A gang of workmen roped together clean and, using a mixture of granite dust, white lead and linseed oil varnish, repair the stern presidents' faces which look down almost 6,700 feet from the top of Mount Rushmore. With a surface 295 feet high and 490 feet wide to cover, the task takes some weeks to complete.

Above right: work on the left eye of Thomas Jefferson, with Gutzon Borglum (left in picture) giving instructions. Below: the second head just before its completion. Right-hand page: cleaning and repairing the enormous heads.

Pages 200–201: Mount Rushmore in evening sunlight. From left: Washington, Jefferson, Theodore Roosevelt, Lincoln.

Mysterious ravine
THE GRAND CANYON

'My name is Lopez de Cárdenas and I have this to report: suddenly the ground under my feet stopped. I looked down and saw an abyss, so deep and so mighty that I cannot find words to describe it. Below at the foot of the ravine gleamed the Red River, the Rio Colorado . . .

Garcia Lopez de Cárdenas was the first white man to describe the Grand Canyon. A member of an expedition led by his fellow countryman Vasquez de Coronado, he was looking for gold and found a natural wonder. It was in 1542 that Cárdenas made his report but over 300 years passed before the mysterious ravine was more closely examined. In 1869 Major J. W. Powell, an American, undertook a daring river journey from the Green River to the Virgin

River and the book he subsequently wrote about this adven[ture] became famous. The Canyon, which is joined by numerous le[sser] ravines, is 217 miles long and between 4,000 and 5,000 feet d[eep] depending on the level of the plateau which it bisects. It c[ould] accommodate the spires of Cologne Cathedral stacked one on [top] of the other ten times over. The width of the wedge-shaped gr[oove] varies between 21 feet and 18 miles. At the bottom the river [bed] which is up to 295 feet wide forms only a narrow channel, a ca[ñon] (in Spanish, cañon).

Through this canyon the leisurely Colorado, sparkling in [its] depths like a silvery little stream, flows to the Gulf of California. [It is] only at high water, when the river rises by dozens of feet, that

206

begin to understand how the Colorado managed over a period
illions of years to make its bed so deep in the earth's crust. It is
med that during the Eozoic Age, that is some 50,000,000 years
the whole Colorado plateau rose considerably. In addition,
e appears to have been a particularly strong influx of water,
cially during the Ice Age. Water and the rubble carried with it
ed through the soft stone, creating a ravine-type river bed.
use of the aridity the steep sides did not erode into a broad
fortable valley but retained instead their ancient precipitousness.
rock walls, towers and peaks descending into the dizzy depths
v provide a geological object lesson more impressive than
hing one could imagine. All the formations from the Cambrian

right through to the Tertiary period are represented in this gigantic
exposition. The surfaces of bare rock are spectacularly and in-
comparably colourful.

'If I were an American,' said the English novelist J. B. Priestley, 'I
would ask myself about everything else in this country: is it good
enough to exist in the same country as the Grand Canyon?'

**On an Indian trail (above) one can ride through the Canyon. Left-
hand page: like a little stream, the Colorado meanders through the
Canyon (left). Below right: diagram of the Grand Canyon from an
old geography book. Above right: a Navaho Indian.**

the largest telescope in the world

MOUNT PALOMAR

On 5,500-foot-high Mount Palomar in California there is a shining dome which is visible for miles. During the day the 134-foot-high dome is shut; it is only at night that the immense hemisphere begins silently to rotate and a broad aperture opens up to reveal a conglomeration of pipes, struts and supports. The giant telescope of Mount Palomar starts its work. Thanks to its famous 200-inch reflector one can look deep into space, even as far as galaxies lying many million light years away. With this, the largest telescope in the world, it is possible to examine a burning candle at a distance of 12,000 miles.

The astronomer's telescope is a relatively new invention. The first telescopes of the seventeenth century led to the discovery of three moons of Jupiter and enabled astronomers to examine the stars of the Milky Way. Over the centuries attempts were made to build larger and larger lens telescopes (refractors), but it was virtually impossible to make a lens with a diameter of more than about three feet. Lenses of this size are difficult to cut. Moreover, there is a danger that they might warp because they are supported only round the edges by the tube of the telescope.

The idea of using the much wider properties of the concave mirror was put forward as early as the seventeenth century, and thus the mirror-telescope (reflector) was developed. Since mirrors, unlike lenses, do not have to be freely suspended but can be supported across their whole surface, attempts could be made to produce larger and, therefore, much more powerful telescopes. In 1901 a 23-inch mirror was made in the USA. Then in 1917 a $7\frac{1}{2}$ foot reflector, the Hooker Telescope at the Mount Wilson Observatory, was built.

The director of the Wilson Observatory at that time was the astronomer George Ellery Hale (1868–1939) who, amongst other achievements, proved the connection between the appearance of magnetic fields and sunspots. Hale was keen to build a telescope with a $24\frac{1}{2}$ foot mirror. This, however, proved to be too ambitious and a 16 foot mirror had to suffice—even that was difficult enough to produce. The Rockefeller Foundation made a donation of 6,000,000 dollars for its development.

No one had any experience of making a mirror of this size. The experiments conducted by General Electric using quartz glass consumed 639,000 dollars but did not result in anything that could be used. Then the Corning Glassworks

The 134-foot-high building of the Mount Palomar Observatory with the dome closed.

209

attempted to produce a mirror out of pyrex. Starting with smaller mirrors, they gradually worked up to the required size. The first attempt failed because the enormous heat used in its manufacture (1,350 degrees C) distorted it but the second attempt (2 December 1934) was successful.

The mirror had to be left for eight months to cool down. Then the 20-ton disc was moved to Pasadena where the laborious task of grinding began. In November 1947, thirteen years after it was moulded, the ground and polished mirror was transported to the observatory on a specially laid road and put into place. Another three years went by before the giant telescope of Mount Palomar was fully operational.

The 500-ton telescope tracks the movement of the stars with consummate ease, and all that is needed to set it in motion is a 60-watt electric motor.

Lord Rosse's giant telescope (below), a forerunner of Palomar. Below right: the gigantic mirror before it was put into place. Above right: dome with aperture open for observation. Right-hand-page: the Hale Telescope, weighing about 500 tons (below); photograph of the Orion nebula which lies 1,300 light years away.

210

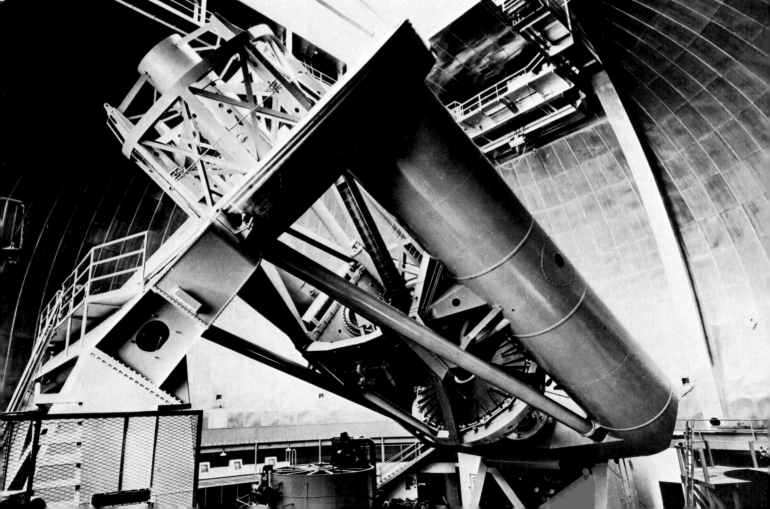

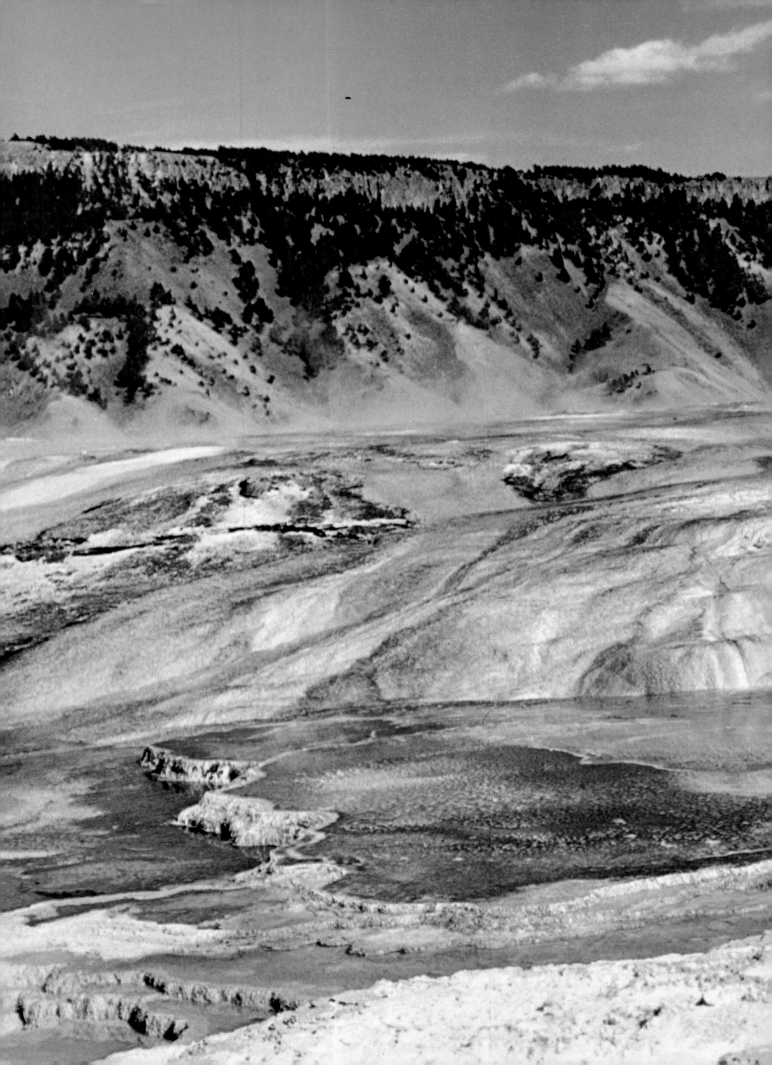

america's wonderland

YELLOWSTONE NATIONAL PARK

'At first a few jets of water spurt out of the opening. It is like an overheated engine about to blow a valve. From the depths we hear a wailing and groaning, as if giant forces were anxious to prevent the outburst, but the superior strength of the steam prevails and suddenly a column of steam rises high into the air quickly followed by a jet of water 150 to 160 feet high, broad as a wall and with a scalding temperature of over 100 degrees C. As quickly as it rose up it subsides again—the whole process has lasted only four minutes. Once again there is calm over the crack in the ground where subterranean forces play their giant game.'

This is how Hermann Dalton, who visited Yellowstone National Park at the turn of the century, described an eruption of the Old Faithful geyser. Of the 10,000 or more hot springs, 'Old Faithful'—so named by General Henry D. Washburn who discovered it because of its punctual eruptions every sixty-five minutes—is the main attraction for the public in a park which could hardly be described as wanting for natural wonders. Over 25,000 eruptions of the hot spring have been recorded in the last eighty-five years and, apart from one or two minor deviations, Old Faithful has always been on time. With each eruption the geyser spits about 10,000 gallons of water into the air, which are then absorbed by the Firehole River.

The centre of the 3,500-square-mile national park, established in 1872 and thus the oldest in the USA, is a plateau of volcanic origin lying at a height of 6,500 to 7,800 feet in the Rocky Mountains. There have been no active volcanoes here since the Tertiary period. Instead, there is a vast and varied assortment of thermal springs. Some look like basins filled with water; from some bubbling water flows over snow white, yellow, brown or orange-yellow limestone terraces. There are also mud springs 'gruesome and repulsive, as if they had been brought here from Dante's Inferno ... Here and there the muddy ground rises up like the thick pap of a lime pit; dirty steaming bubbles form which burst and throw out muddy water; but all this in such great contours as if the head of one of the damned wanted to rise out of the pool.' (Dalton).

Yellowstone Park has still more to offer. In the middle lies Yellowstone Lake; up to 300 feet deep and with an area of about 140 square miles, it is the largest mountain lake in North America. The Yellowstone River flows through the area in a 24-mile-long loop. Over a period of centuries it has eaten into the volcanic rock to form a 1,000-foot-deep canyon. Two falls interrupt its course; at the larger of the two the river plunges from a height of 300 feet into the ravine below which is particularly narrow at this point.

The use of the national park is controlled by strict regulations which are enforced—as in all the other parks in the USA—by the rangers—park keepers equipped with police powers. Initially, cavalry units of the US army were responsible for keeping law and order. Fishing in Yellowstone Lake is permitted but the well-being of the rich wild life, which includes, among others, bear, red deer, elk, mountain sheep and bison, is jealously protected by the rangers.

Above right: waterfall and canyon of the Yellow River in the national park. Below: Old Faithful during an eruption - punctual as a clock. Right-hand page: colour magic of nature, demonstrated by water containing minerals (above). Bottom row from left: steam between bushes and trees; sulphur lake; stone terraces built up by the Minerva geyser.

Pages 212-213: 'Great Terrace' near Mammoth Hot Springs.

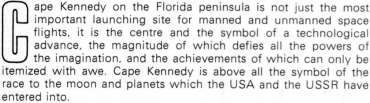

ape Kennedy on the Florida peninsula is not just the most important launching site for manned and unmanned space flights, it is the centre and the symbol of a technological advance, the magnitude of which defies all the powers of the imagination, and the achievements of which can only be itemized with awe. Cape Kennedy is above all the symbol of the race to the moon and planets which the USA and the USSR have entered into.

The age of space travel began—after the first trials with rockets for investigating the atmosphere—in October 1957 with the launching of Sputnik I, the first artificial earth satellite, by the USSR. After that countless unmanned spacecraft were launched—research

satellites designed to gather specific scientific information, c munications satellites for the transcontinental relay of radio television programmes, weather satellites for the observation of overall weather pattern and finally space probes for the explora of interplanetary space.

The experience gained from unmanned spacecraft provided foundations for manned space flight. The immediate aim, wl the USA recently achieved through the Apollo Programme, wa land men on the surface of the moon; their ultimate aim, accorc to James E. Webb, chief of NASA (National Aeronautics and Sp Administration), is 'the development and production of that sp travel system which will be needed in the years to come'. All

nned space flights which have so far been carried out—the first
s on 12 April 1961 when the Soviet cosmonaut Yuri Gagarin
bited the earth; the second, manned by the American Alan
epard, was three weeks later—are to be assessed as preparations
the flight to the moon and other planets.

The USA began with the Mercury programme. Over the period
61 to 1963 the Americans fired six manned rockets, each weighing
on, into orbit round the earth. The Gemini link-up programme started
1965 with the first American 'twin flight', involving astronauts
ssom and Young. The two-man capsule used weighed three tons.

to the close of this programme in November 1966 ten space
hts had taken place, the longest lasting 330 hours. For the planned

moon landing the docking technique, that is the meeting and joining
up of two spacecraft while in orbit round the earth, which was tested
in this programme, was of decisive importance. For the first time,

**Left-hand page from above: assembling Saturn I rockets; transporting
a Saturn rocket on the Tennessee River; control room for the Saturn
tests. Centre: Saturn launching pad under construction. Above:
launching of a Titan II rocket on 3 June 1965 with astronauts
McDivitt and White (Gemini Programme).**

**Pages 216-217: Cape Kennedy with the 575-foot-high assembly
room for rockets and the special road leading to the launching pad.**

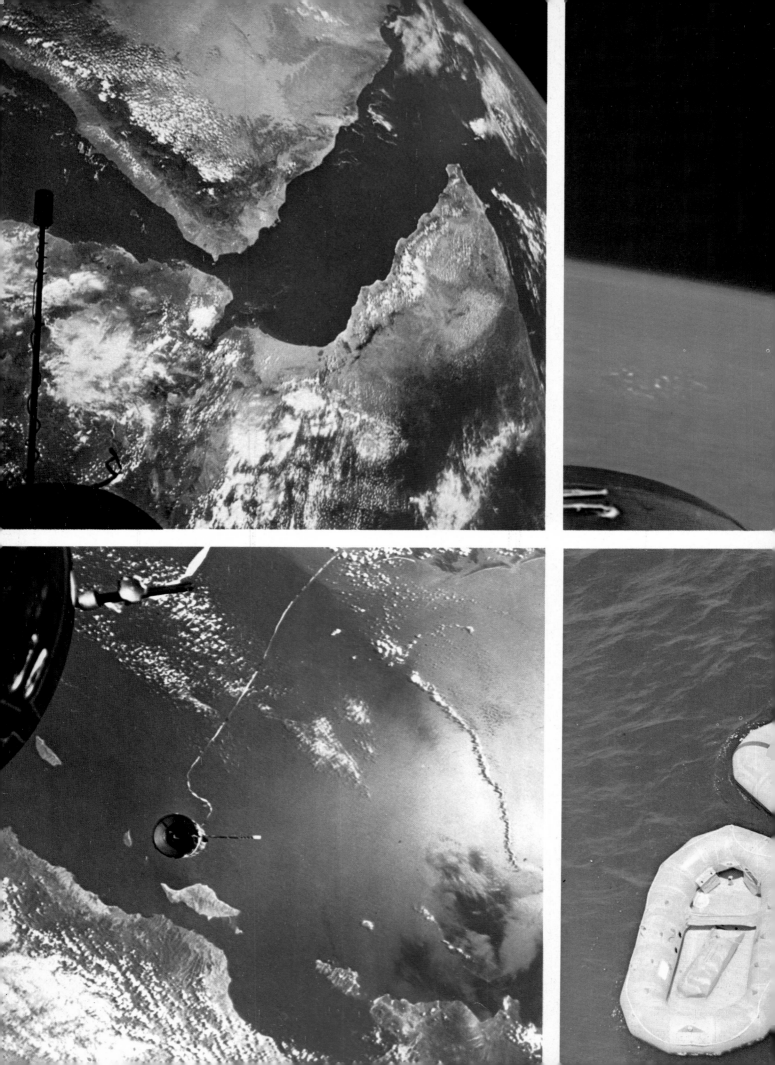

in December 1965, the spacecrafts Gemini VI and VII managed to come within a foot of each other.

Compared with the financial outlay, the organization and the expertise involved in the third American space flight series, the Apollo Programme, the efforts and expense of earlier years, which look so enormous in isolation, fade far into the background. For the realization of the project to get three people to the moon the American government engaged about 20,000 firms and some 40,000 people. The programme cost over £6,000,000 a day. Today the space travel business is already one of the largest industries in the USA. The work not only serves the immediate purposes of space research but also has a surprisingly wide and productive bearing on many other branches of applied science. From programme to programme the space capsules have become steadily larger and heavier, and the rockets more and more powerful. The 100-foot-long Atlas rockets of the Mercury Programme were capable of carrying a capsule weighing up to 1 ton; the 90-foot-long Titan II rockets of the Gemini Programme propelled capsules weighing up to three tons. For the Apollo Programme two types of Saturn rockets were constructed: one with a length of 120 feet capable of carrying 10 tons; the other 140 feet long and able to carry 18 tons. Provisionally, the limit is set by the 364-foot-long Saturn V rocket, a giant rocket as heavy as a small cruiser, with a load capacity of 126 tons and a thrust power of 150,000,000 h.p., built at a unit cost of £50,000,000.

Cape Kennedy is equipped to handle this monster, and also even larger rockets. On Merit Island, one of the largest buildings in the world was conjured up, an assembly room for rockets. The number of workshops, testing centres, control centres, observation rooms and assembly shops and the amount of testing equipment is inconceivably large. The byword in assembling the gigantic tower-like rockets is absolute precision. 'The individual components are ground to one two-thousandth of a millimetre; electronic switches put together under the microscope, wires one eighth of the thickness of a woman's hair automatically soldered. In some air-conditioned workshops special air filters create an almost antiseptic purity. The control installations give out an alarm if specks of dust less than one thousandth of a millimetre in size penetrate the room.' (Heinrich Rieker).

A caterpillar transporter, the largest in the world, was constructed for the transportation of the moon rockets. Saturn V, comprising gantry and space capsule, was brought to the launching pad near the coast on a road specially constructed for this purpose with an eight-foot-thick track of reinforced concrete. The Apollo capsule consisted of three parts. In the command module the three astronauts travelled to the moon and went into orbit around it. Leaving one man in the command module, the other two climbed into the lunar excursion module and descended to the surface of the moon. They remained there for some hours; Neil Armstrong became the first man to set foot on the moon. After coupling with the command module, the third part of the spacecraft, the motor, came into operation, bringing the astronauts back to earth. On a later Apollo mission, the occupants of the lunar module took their own self-propelled vehicle, in which they were able to cruise gently over the pitted surface of earth's ancient sister.

Left-hand page: the Red Sea (left) with the southern tip of the Arabian Peninsula, Ethiopia and Somalia photographed during the Gemini II flight. Gemini II with attached Agena rockets flying over La Paz Bay on the Californian peninsula. Astronaut White during the first American space flight with Gemini IV (above). Splash-down of the Gemini IV capsule with White and McDivitt.

The most famous suspension bridge in the world

THE GOLDEN GATE BRIDGE

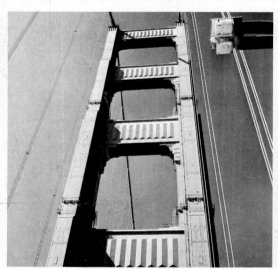

After Los Angeles, San Francisco, the 'Queen of the Pacific', is the largest city on the west coast of North America. It lies on a peninsula, which, shaped like an enormous bolt, separates the greater part of the 55-mile-long and 12-mile-wide San Francisco Bay from the open sea. A channel not much more than half a mile wide connects the bay with the Pacific Ocean. Its narrowest point is the famous Golden Gate spanned by the Golden Gate Bridge. Until 1965 it held the record as the longest suspension bridge in the world but was then overtaken by the Verrazano Narrows Bridge, in New York, which is fifty-nine feet longer. Originally, there was only a Franciscan mission, founded in the eighteenth century on the hilly peninsula. In 1848 the number of inhabitants in the

settlement which had become established not far from the mis was about 500. Two years later it had already reached 25,000 in the meantime gold had been found in Sacramento. Prospec rushed in their thousands to San Francisco which became a ra[expanding centre for the coarse and unruly gold diggers. The e expanding town—by the turn of the century the number of habitants had increased to more than 300,000—soon spread as as the southern and eastern coasts of the bay. It soon became evi that a bridge would have to be built in order to avoid lengthy det along the coast road, and the plan for the Oakland Suspen Bridge was put forward on which work began in 1905. Ove miles long, it was constructed from over 185,000 tons of steel

,000 tons of cement. A giant amongst bridges, it was considerably
ier than the bridge on which it had been modelled, Brooklyn
ge in New York.

year later, on 18 April 1906, San Francisco was struck by a
strous earthquake quickly followed by a fire. The city was almost
pletely destroyed and 452 people died under the debris. In the
s that followed the work of rebuilding the city—on a larger and
e splendid scale than before—began. During the thirties the
eme to span the Golden Gate with a single-span suspension
ge was discussed. Many specialists considered it impossible to
d a bridge with such an enormous span (4,200 feet). Above all
were afraid that a new earthquake could destroy the supports.

However, the Golden Gate Bridge, which was altogether $1\frac{1}{2}$ miles
long, was built. The 36-inch-thick main cable was hung on supports
688 feet high and to it the 78-foot-wide roadway was secured
In 1937 it was ready to be opened—'a splendid monument in a splendid
panorama of city, sea and mountains'. Today, it seems the bridge is
so strong that it can support a second carriageway.

**Above: Oakland Suspension Bridge (Bay Bridge) over San Francisco
Bay. Left-hand page: the Golden Gate with the Golden Gate Bridge.
Bottom row from left: view of the bridge from one of the 688-foot-
high supports; building a pylon: cross-section of the main cable,
which is one yard thick.**

Chicago, a city not exactly lacking in skyscrapers, has a new landmark —Marina City, two impressive skyscraper blocks over 550 feet high and 100 feet in diameter. These sixty-storey tower blocks, nicknamed 'corncobs' or 'grain silos' by the local inhabitants, are composed of flats suspended from a 40-foot-wide reinforced concrete core which houses the lifts, stairs, refuse chutes and services.

Every floor is divided into sixteen equal sectors, each with its own balcony. The sectors are variously combined, some flats occupying one, some one and a half and some two and a half sectors. An average apartment, comprising hall, bedroom, bathroom, kitchen and living room, has an area of about 325 square feet.

Luxury is evident everywhere, with refrigerator, electric cooker, air-conditioning and built-in cupboards as standard fittings. The two blocks, with their 912 apartments inhabited by some 2,000 people, form in themselves a small town

The corncob houses of Chicago
MARINA CITY

whose needs are catered for by special restaurants, shops, a bank and a travel agency. The ground floor has been provided with mooring space for private motor boats: Lake Michigan can be reached more quickly by boat on the Chicago River than by car on the permanently congested roads. Of course, there is no shortage of parking facilities: the lower floors of both towers provide space for 1,000 vehicles. The flats begin

at the twenty-first floor, and the higher they lie, the more they cost. Marina City is only for the rich. The comfort, the prestigious address, the select location are things that have to be paid for. A bachelor flat costing 150 dollars on the twenty-first floor goes for 220 dollars on the fifty-second floor. The most expensive flat, composed of two and a half sectors, costs about 840 dollars per month in 1967 with garage, heating and light included. Also included in the price is the magnificent view of the second largest city in the USA (over 6,000,000 inhabitants), which stretches for sixty miles along Lake Michigan. Not at a loss for superlatives, the builders claimed that their tower houses are the tallest flats in the world, and not without justification: all taller buildings are office blocks.

The tower flats of Marina City (far left and left) against the city skyline of Chicago – a fascinating subject for photographers (below).

The 'Greece of the New World' is the name given by some historians to the Maya kingdom which is pre-Colombian times extended over the Mexican peninsula and the bordering areas to the south. So far more than 130 places of worship have been excavated in this region; several of them are reminiscent in their size and splendour of the Acropolis in Athens. On first encountering Chichen Itza, the temple city to the north of Yucatan, however, one is strongly reminded of the gigantic buildings at Angkor in Cambodia, the only assembly of colossal ruins more extensive than that of Chichen Itza itself.

The buildings of Chichen Itza were the work of the Maya, who, at the time of the Old Kingdom which lasted from the fifth century BC to the sixth century AD, inhabited southern central America, roughly in the region of Chiapas, Tabasco, Guatemala and Honduras. Then they moved farther north into the heart of the Yucatan peninsula, leaving behind a temple area with enormous terraces and pyramidal buildings. The reason for this migration has never been established. Perhaps the land near the old settlement worked with primitive tools had ceased to be fertile; perhaps an epidemic had broken out; or perhaps there had been a change in the climate.

Whatever the reason, there was little in their new home to encourage them to build towns, for the Maya had moved into an area which was a mixture of bleak limestone scenery and luxuriant primeval forest and in which there was only a limited amount of water. The new temples, therefore, arose near the places where water was to be found. Apart from the metropolis of Chichen Itza, the religious centres of Uxmal and Mayapan became the focal points of the New Empire, and were no less magnificent in their construction than the places that had been abandoned.

It was assumed by Arnold Toynbee that 'There must once have been a time when these extensive public buildings stood in the heart of larger, more densely populated towns; a time when these towns lay in the middle of well cultivated fields', but according to more recent findings that was probably not the case. Chichen Itza was built solely as a place of worship and administrative centre in the form still recognizable today and was inhabited only by the priesthood and aristocracy. The ordinary people did not have stone buildings but lived in wooden huts away from the temple area which they visited only for important religious ceremonies.

The Temple of the Warriors surrounded by the Thousand Pillars at Chichen Itza.

City of ruins in Yucatan
CHICHEN ITZA

By the time the Spanish arrived in the country, Chichen Itza had already fallen into ruins and was gradually being repossessed by the tropical forest. It was not until a hundred years ago that an interest began to be shown in the decaying Maya temples and Chichen Itza began to be excavated and restored. Many of the ancient inscriptions and symbols could be deciphered, and the theory that the Maya had lived in fear under a dictatorial religion based on the calendar was confirmed. Complicated calculations by the priests determined the most favourable dates for all decisions affecting the life of the peoples. All periods of time—comparable with our weeks or months—were deified. The priests left amazingly accurate calculations about the course of Venus and impending solar eclipses but, on other hand, the Maya knew nothing of the wheel, the plough o measurement of weight.

On closer examination archaeologists discovered in most of buildings of Chichen Itza stylistic influences which did not bel to the Maya culture. During the early thirteenth century the the Mayan tribe responsible for Chichen Itza, were conquered Toltec people from central Mexico. It was they who built the l pyramid (*El Castillo*) dedicated to Kukulkan, which lies at the ce of the area, and the Temple of the Warriors surrounded by Thousand Pillars. The Caracol, a circular building, which served

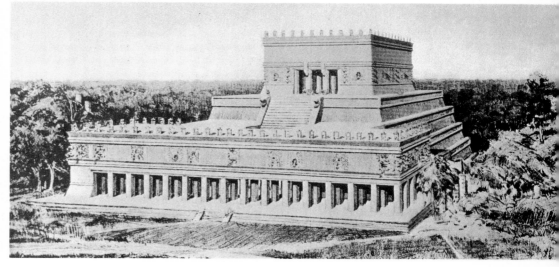

in observatory, and the pitch for ball games on which the holy ne of pelota was played are also evidence of Toltec architecture ch at Chichen Itza became mingled with the traditional forms of Maya. This juxtaposition operated even in the representations ne gods: besides Toltec-Aztec gods, such as Quetzalcoatl, the va rain gods were not forgotten.

nyone visiting Chichen Itza should not miss seeing the larger he two walls near which the temple complex was built. The dle-like spring (Cenote) was of great religious importance. In r to placate the gods jewellery, weapons and incense were thrown o the well, and festively adorned maidens sacrificed to the rain-

dispensing deities. For the Toltecs rain was vital. 'No rain—no corn— no life!' as the Maya guide explains to people visiting the holy well of Chichen Itza.

Left page: entrance to the Temple of Warriors with snakes' heads (above). Façade of the 'nunnery' (below). Centre: the Temple of Kukulkan ('El Castillo') in the centre of the town (above) was linked by a road to the holy well (below). Right: one of the flights of steps on the Temple of Kukulkan (above); reconstruction of the Temple of the Warriors (below).

Nerve of world shipping

THE PANAMA CANAL

The idea for a link between the Carribean Sea and the Pacific Ocean is an old one. The Spanish conquistadors of Central and South America came to grips with this problem as long ago as the beginning of the sixteenth century. The Emperor Charles V was farsighted enough to understand the great political and economic advantages of a canal in the isthmus of Panama and in 1524 he had the first sketches for the bold project drawn up. But over 350 years passed before the building of the water route from sea to sea was systematically tackled.

Today, fifty years after the opening of the Panama Canal, the shipping route through the Panama isthmus is, after the Suez Canal, the most important direct link between two oceans. In 1952 a total of 6,600 passages in both directions was recorded. Fifteen years later this number had more than doubled. The figures of the Panama Canal Company for 1966 recorded 13,300 passages. The toll for an ocean-going merchant ship is about £2,900 which is not cheap — but the reduction in mileage has to be borne in mind. By travelling through the Panama Canal the journey from New York to Yokohama, for example, is reduced by 7,000 sea miles (about 8,000 land miles).

The idea of a canal through the isthmus of Panama came under serious consideration in the middle of the last century. Fearing that so valuable a trump card might slip from their hand in the power game, the USA and Great Britain signed an agreement in 1850 to secure strict neutrality for the territory of the proposed canal. But that the agreement stood on weak ground soon became apparent.

Encouraged by the great success of the Suez Canal project, which had been concluded in 1869, France announced her interest and promoted the establishment of the Compagnie Universelle du Canal Interocéanique de Panama. The company, directed by Ferdinand de Lesseps, the engineer of the Suez Canal, acquired the concession and in 1879 work on the project began. But ten years later the company went bankrupt and all efforts to put the concern, which had fallen further into disrepute because of a corruption scandal, back on a sound economic footing were unsuccessful. De Lesseps foundered on the colossal problems of finance, organization and hygiene posed by the building of the canal.

The next developments might have been anticipated. The United States, which two decades earlier was still in danger of being left behind in the bid for power in Central America, took a hand. First of all the Americans secured sole rights in the building of the canal through two agreements (1901 and 1902). Then in 1903 they assisted in the separation of the Panamanian area from Colombia and the proclamation of the *Republica de Panama*. The new republic rewarded the USA with the rights of sovereignty over the canal zone, at the same time granting the American administration a strip of land five miles wide on each side of the canal—altogether a territory of 552 square miles. The way for the unhindered execution of the great building plan was now open. In 1906 the American Congress granted the capital necessary to start and engineer George Washington Goethals (1858–1928) was put in charge of the building operations.

It took seven years to dig the channel through the isthmus. Progress was often hampered for weeks at a time by enormous landslides. On the bottom of the excavated canal bed six or seven railway tracks ran side by side. Millions of tons of rock had to be blasted and carried away. In 1910 alone over 15,000,000 pounds of explosives were used. Yellow fever and malaria took tens of thousands of lives among the workmen.

Shortly after the outbreak of war in Europe, the first ship sailed through the canal on 15 August 1914. Six years later, on 12 June 1920, the waterway, by now virtually finished, was officially opened to world shipping.

With an average width of 655 feet, the canal is 40 miles long from coast to coast and 50 miles long from deep water to deep water. From the harbours of Colon and Cristobal on the Atlantic side, the

On the Pacific side the stepped Miraflores locks compensate for the difference in level between the Pacific and Lake Gatun.

course of the canal is interrupted first by the Gatun locks, a three-stage system of locks which raises the ships to the level of Lake Gatun, a large, artificial lake formed by damming a river and lying 85 feet above sea level.

After the passage through the lake (the route is indicated by numerous lighthouses and marker buoys) ships then travel in a south-easterly direction to the lower section of the waterway, where they pass through the Gaillard Cut and the locks and sluices of Pedro Miguel and Miraflores, before reaching the exit (which again lies correspondingly lower than Lake Gatun) on the Pacific side. On average the passage through the canal lasts eight hours.

President Theodore Roosevelt once said: 'Without the initiative, the wealth of ideas, the ideals and the dollars of the Americans, the canal would never have been built.' His statement is perfectly true, and America's needs were the motive for the canal's construction. A third of all the ships that pass through the canal fly the United States flag.

The Gaillard Cut, a mountain cut, was one of the most difficult sections of the canal to build (above). Centre: ship leaving a lock. Below: cross-section of the canal. Right-hand page: the Thatcher Ferry Bridge crosses the canal near Panama (above). Below from left: excavation work on the canal using a steam shovel (1911); cemetery for 56,000 workers who died of yellow fever and malaria during the construction of the canal; Gatun dam which regulates the level of water in the canal in the region of Lake Gatun.

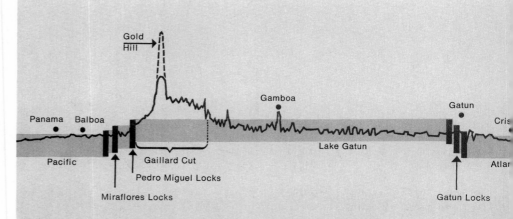

The most beautiful city in the world
RIO DE JANEIRO

The full name of the city with 4,000,000 inhabitants which has been called the most beautiful in the world is São Sebastiao do Rio de Janeiro: St Sebastian of the January River. When on 20 January 1500 the Portuguese with six caravels moored below the famous Sugar Loaf Mountain in order to drive away the French, they mistook the bay for the mouth of a river and named the supposed river after the current month. Fifteen years later, when the city was founded, the name was retained and simply enlarged with the name of St Sebastian. In the course of time the full name became abbreviated to Rio de Janeiro or simply Rio.

What gives Rio the right to the pretentious title of the most beautiful city in the world? 'There may be more beautiful lakes t the Bay of Rio which has been likened to an alpine lake,' traveller has remarked, 'naturally, there are higher mountains, tinguished by even more beautiful contours than those wh enclose this bay; there are larger cities than Rio, and there other cities in the tropics that lie in equally magnificent countrys But there is no other combination on our planet of sea and islar of bold alpine chains and city panoramas with everything clot in the most magnificent tropical splendour, such as that offe by the bay of Rio de Janeiro!'

Another traveller, A. E. Johann, is of a different opinion. Not

nense boulevards, not the mountains in and between and behind
, not the 80-foot-high statue of Christ standing high above the
, nor the regiments of skyscrapers in the Copacabanca district
in his view, the most beautiful things in Rio, 'but the girls on the
ch, on the light glittering strand with the silvery shimmering of
Atlantic, this enticing beach, which softly curves for miles below
skyscrapers.'
Rio is, one could go on, of special charm when observed from
bat. Spreading across the 110-mile bay, its best side can be seen
n Corcovado, the 2,300-foot-high mountain with the statue of
ist, or from the Sugar Loaf, which can be ascended in a cable
way. Rio is at its most beautiful when darkness begins to fall

and the lights gleam like strings of pearls.

From 1763 until the opening of Brasilia in the year 1960—almost
200 years—Rio de Janeiro was the capital of Brazil. It appears that
the city has easily overcome the loss of its status as capital, and it
has never ceased to be the spiritual centre of the country.

**Above: packed beach at the famous Copacabana with its palatial
hotels. Left-hand page: view of the Bay of Rio with the Corcovado
(above) on which the 82-foot-high statue of Christ stands (left).
Below right: view of the Bay of Rio at the turn of the century.**

Pages 236–237: view of Rio de Janeiro from the Corcovado.

Blue-print metropolis

BRASILIA

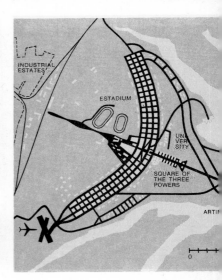

The first discussions about transferring the capital of Brazil from the coast to the interior took place in 1825. In 1851 the conception was formalized in a general way but nothing came of it until 1956 when President Juscelino Kubitschek de Oliveira took steps to have the scheme put into effect. The major part of the project was to be completed in four years—a breathtaking schedule if it were maintained.

It started with the establishment of a state building company Novacap. The appointment of chief architect went to Oscar Niemeyer who declared himself for 'unlimited plastic freedom' and swore 'Never to fall into the hitherto customary banal style of [public] building.' The third creative force in the making of Brasilia

was Lucio Costa who designed the general layout for the new cap His plan was in the form of a cross with a main axis 3½ miles l and 370 yards wide (five times as wide as the Avenue des Cha Elysées in Paris), on which the public buildings were to be c structed. Crossing this magnificent avenue was to be the be shaped residential axis with living complexes (Quadras) c prising blocks of flats, business premises, schools, churches recreational areas.

The first building to be erected was the president's residence, Alvorado Palace, with its famous triangular pillars, which was b over an artificial lake. The Square of the Three Powers contains government and judicial buildings, two skyscrapers each twe

…t storeys high, and a long low building with a saucer-shaped … which contains the house of representatives while the Senate … beneath a dome at the other end. The Planalto Palace (seat of …ernment), the law courts, the imposing ministry blocks adjoining … side facing the city centre, and the as yet unfinished cathedral, …eaflike bundle of concrete rods, also stand here.

…he architects left nothing to chance, and an enormous university, …ools, museums, theatres, banks, hotels, hospitals, swimming …ns were all provided for in the original plans. On 21 April 1960 …silia was ready to be opened as planned. The comments were …ed. John Dos Passos called the city an 'inverted Pompeii'; …rs spoke of test-tube architecture, of a drawing-board metro-

polis in which nobody would want to live. The Brazilians, however, seem to have got used to their still unfinished capital. There are now over 300,000 people living there. André Malraux was right when he called Brasilia *La Capitale d'Espoire*, the Capital of Hope.

Above: view from Planalto Palace (seat of government) of the congress buildings. Left-hand page: ministry blocks (above left); sculpture in the Square of the Three Powers (above right); children's hospital (centre left); Kubitschek memorial on the city museum (centre right); presidential palace (below left); building plan of Brasilia (below right). Pages 240–241: centre of Brasilia with congress buildings (left).

If the waterfalls of the Iguaçu River lay in one of the great tourist areas, in a part of the world opened up by modern means of transport, and not in an almost inaccessible primeval forest in South America, it would be impossible to defend them against the onslaught of hordes of tourists, and the roll of visitors would long have exceeded that of the Niagara Falls. There are, of course, small villages on both banks of the river—Foz do Iguaçu in the Brazilian coffee state of Paraná, Porto Iguazú in the Argentinian province of Misiones—which owe their very existence to the famous falls. Nevertheless, as a tourist attraction the Iguaçu Falls have managed to retain a certain rarity value—much to the approval of many conservationists. As there has so far been no move to convert the masses of water into hydroelectric power, this wonder in the tropics at the corner of three countries—Brazil, Argentina and Paraguay all converge here—can still be seen in its original unspoiled state.

The deep and turbulent Iguaçu is a tributary of the 2,900-mile-long Paraná, which, united with the Rio Uruguay and other rivers, eventually forms the Rio de la Plata which flows into the Atlantic at Buenos Aires. The source of the Iguaçu lies near Curitiba in the rugged coastal region of the Serra do Mar. In spite of countless rapids large stretches of the 460-mile-long river are navigated by motor boats and steamers. In the upper reaches of the Paraná there are several waterfalls, the most impressive being the Guaíra Falls, beyond which the river flows on in a deep ravine along the border between Paraguay and Brazil. All the tributaries which flow into the Paraná along this stretch have to descend into the ravine, and so the entire reach is full of cataracts and waterfalls. The most beautiful of these are the Iguaçu Falls, fourteen miles above the confluence with the Paraná.

For years the Brazilians have numbered the Iguaçu Falls, which like the Niagara Falls are bisected by national boundaries, among the wonders of the world. They are also careful to point out that they are not, in fact, just one solitary fall but twenty-one separate falls, all thundering down over a width of about $1\frac{1}{2}$ miles into the narrow gorge 230 to 260 feet below. The thundering of the falls can be heard fifteen miles away. One of the two main falls has etched a horseshoe-shaped recess at the edge of the precipice. When on clear days the sun's rays shatter the spray above the famous Garganta do Diabo (the Devil's Throat), a rainbow with a span of over 130 yards is formed. The Falls are at their most impressive during the rainy season when some 140,000,000 tons of water an hour pour over the falls—seven times the volume of Niagara.

The first reports of the Iguaçu Falls reached Europe relatively late —in the sixteenth century. At that time the Jesuits had started to build up their famous Indian Republic in the state of Paraná and Paraguay. The Guarnari, who were their main concern, were grouped into communities which were divided into 'reductions'. The Jesuits organized farming, arranged workshops, were at pains to better the living conditions of the Indians. They administered a kind of democracy and provided the necessary connections for foreign trade. Later they also set up Indian armed forces.

Other white men had no reason to visit the Indian settlements. When tradesmen came to examine goods, they were received and entertained by the priests in reception houses far outside the villages. This isolation from European civilization was one of the basic principles of the Jesuit republic. The missionaries deliberately avoided the areas at the mouths of great rivers which were accessible to white settlers and went into the unexplored interior. Their work began in an area cut off by cataracts, waterfalls and rapids.

Father Sepp from the Tyrol wrote: 'Our missionaries are all of the opinion that God created these waterfalls and rapids for the use of our poor Indians, for the Spaniards in their insatiable greed for money have come as far as this with their large ships, but no farther. Up to the present time they have not reached our people.' In later

Over a width of about $1\frac{3}{4}$ miles the waters of the Iguaçu, divided into 21 separate falls, plunge 250 feet into the ravine below.

tries meet

years, however, that was to change. Portuguese adventurers called *Bandeirantes* found the reductions an easily overpowered source of slaves. Tens of thousands of Indians were dragged off to the slave market. Eventually the Jesuits fled with the last 12,000 Guarani down the Iguaçu on the way to the Paraná. The waterfalls were the first great obstacle.

'One tried to let the boats go down the falls: they arrived in pieces at the bottom. It took a week before the falls could be circumvented and the rebuilding of the boats taken in hand. Only a very small proportion found room in the boats: the others went on through the forest in various groups, and grave after grave marked their passage, for they were beset by hunger and disease.' (von Hauff). Their flight brought peace for only a few years. The Portuguese and Spaniards expelled the Jesuits. The Indians returned to the forests; the missions decayed. After 150 years the Utopia in the forest came to an end.

The name of the Argentinian province Misiones, the district bordering on the Iguaçu Falls, is a reminder of this experiment, the authors of which were too far ahead of their time.

Above: waterfall at the Devil's Throat. Below: the Iguaçu at the bottom of the gorge. Left-hand page: three views of this wonder of nature amid the tropical forests – waterfalls as far as the eye can see.

Inca refuge
MACHU PICCHU

When the Spanish conquistadors under Pizarro destroyed many of the Inca people and murdered Atahualpa, their last ruler, the rest of the people fled to a distant mountain fortress in the Andes. From there they persistently attacked the conquistadors for thirty-nine years, while the Spaniards searched in vain for their secret refuge. When the last Incas had gone the mountain fortress of Machu Picchu, an eagle's nest of gigantic stones, was deserted. It was rediscovered only a few decades ago although its existence had long been known.

Blood and gold directed the course of the 168 soldiers with whom Captain-General Francisco Pizarro set out to conquer the Inca kingdom for the Spanish throne. He arrived at an opportune moment. The last sole ruler, Huayna Capac, had divided the kingdom between his sons Atahualpa and Huascar. The two successors quarrelled and a civil war flared up from which Atahualpa emerged the victor; he imprisoned his brother in Cuzco, the famous Inca capital—its name means 'navel of the world'. At Cajamarca, a northern city, Atahualpa awaited the band of Spaniards.

On 25 November 1532 Pizarro appeared outside the town. In open combat his troops could hardly have prevailed against the 30,000 or more battle-tried Inca warriors, but Pizarro enticed the ruler into his headquarters and made him prisoner. That day 4,000 Indians lost their lives. Atahualpa, having observed the Spaniards' lust for gold, tried to buy his freedom from Pizarro. 'He offered to fill the room in which he was imprisoned as far as his fingertips could reach with gold. In return the Spaniards were to give him his freedom.' (Francisco de Xerez).

Pizarro agreed. Countless gold treasures were showered on the Spaniards, but in spite of that the Inca never saw freedom again. The Captain-General had him strangled—for no substantial reason except that he feared him, but before he died Atahualpa cursed his murderers. The curse of the Inca was fulfilled. Within a short time all the parties to the deed, including Pizarro, assassinated by his colleagues, suffered gruesome deaths. Molten gold was poured into the eye sockets of the chaplain who had christened the Inca 'Francisco Atahualpa' shortly before his execution—Pizarro had acted as godfather. The Captain-General had installed Manco Capac, one of Atahualpa's brothers, as the new Inca. But the sham Inca was no willing tool of the Spaniards: he set himself at the head of the enraged Indians and led them against their oppressors. After an indescribable massacre the Spaniards emerged victorious. Manco Capac retreated with his followers, including many 'sun-daughters', virgins

in flames. Again and again the Spaniards tried to trace the hiding place of the rebels and they stopped searching only when the attacks ceased because the Inca forces had died out or lost heart for the endless struggle.

In the nineteenth century conquerors, adventurers, gold prospectors and scientists searched for a hidden stronghold but all without success. It was Hiram Bingham, professor of history and leader of an expedition from Yale University, who first tracked down the hideout. On 24 July 1911 he first saw the walls of Machu Picchu overgrown by the vigorous forest. A year later, after long arduous months of burning the vegetation and cutting it back with machetes, he could see the entire area. In front of him lay an enormous flight of terraces and steps—his companions gave up counting the steps after reaching 3,200—and there were walls and towers, streams and temples, graves with numerous sarcophagi and holy stones.

The unique position of the mountain city, which could once have contained 10,000 people, made it clear why neither Spaniards nor explorers had succeeded in finding Machu Picchu. The mountain peak covered with terraced buildings is enclosed on three sides by a steep gorge 2,300 feet deep, containing a vast turbulent river, the Urubamba. On the fourth side access is barred by a mountain ridge. The clever positioning of the walls further improved the natural fortifications. At the time of the Incas there were presumably bridges over the river which could either be drawn in or completely destroyed at times of crisis. Before he could start excavating the deserted city, Hiram Bingham had to construct a makeshift bridge over the Urubamba and install a cableway.

The professor later explained how 'walls of carefully laid stone blocks strengthened the most important points in such a way that the defenders could roll down rocks from the top-most peaks without endangering themselves.' But in fact he found no indication that there specially instructed in religious ritual to, it is believed the mountain fortress, Machu Picchu, once maintained by the Incas as a border fortress against neighbouring tribes. From there, during the decades that followed, he and his successors made countless assaults on the Spaniards, including a prolonged siege of Cuzco, which together with all its splendid buildings and treasures went up

In their flight from the Spanish conquistadors the last of the Incas may have retreated into the impregnable mountain fortress of Machu Picchu. They were never discovered there.

249

had ever been any serious assaults on the city by enemy forces. There are other riddles about the border fortress that still remain unsolved, in spite of the extensive finds of graves and fragments. Why did the last of the Incas finally give up Machu Picchu? Who built the enormous stone walls which, unlike the other buildings of Machu Picchu, do not conform to the Inca style of architecture? How were these heavy stones brought to the mountain which, even without such a load, is barely accessible? Perhaps one day the theory that Machu Picchu was already being used as a fortress thousands of years before the birth of Christ will be substantiated, but explanations are hardly to be expected from Inca sources, because they believed that the world began with the rule of the first Inca.

Right, from top: the 'Princes grave' with sacrificial altar; defence turret with steps cut out of the rock; the famous 'Temple of the Three Windows'; part of the wall made out of enormous blocks of stone laid one on top of the other. Far right: the 'Sun Observatory' – the purpose of this building has still not been explained.

ACKNOWLEDGMENTS

Colour
Anthony-Verlag, Starnberg : Bethmann : 118 ar ; Schlapper : 131 cr ; W. Bayer : 215 bc & br.
Archiv für Kunst und Geschichte, Berlin : 13, 15 bl, 16a, 17b.
Associated Press Picture Service, Frankfurt a.M. : 59bc.
Erich Bauer, Karlsruhe : 11 b, 43 b, 52–53, 168–169, 207.
Bavaria-Verlag, Gauting : Almasy : 139 br, 234 a, 243 ; Max Bickel : 35 a, 54 a ; G. Binanzer : 107 ar ; Karl Droste : 160–161 ; D. Hecker : 238a ; H. Kanus : 68–69, 119 al, 122 bc ; M. Kraft : 87 bl ; Leidmann : 101 b ; Omnia : 164–165 ; M. Pedone : 46 bl, 56–57 ; Z. J. Pivecka : 226–227.
Horst Bergmann, Gütersloh : 43 cl, 96–97.
Klaus Brantl, Munich : 42a, 55 a & b.
Deutsche Luftbild KG, Hamburg : 24–25, 58 a.
dpa-Bild, Frankfurt a.M. : 124–125, 127 (Rauchwetter), 130 (Paolo Koch), 134, 148–149, 151, 170–171 (Schmidt-Wiking), 173 r (Schmidt-Wiking), 188–189, 191, 212–213 (Bernhaut), 216–217, 219 r, 220–221 b.
French Tourist Office, Frankfurt a.M. : 84–85.
Roland Gööck, Munich : 70 r, 71 bl.
W. Gontscharoff, Munich : 28–29, 31 c, 64–65, 72–73, 74, 75, 76–77, 78 al & r, 79, 80–81, 83 a, bl & br.
Güntherpress (Henle), Lübeck : 47, 88–89, 107 bl.
Ray Halin : 186.
Hans Huber, Garmisch-Partenkirchen : 39 bc ; 40–41. 43 al & ar, 59 r, 100 a, 108–109, 112–113, 115.
Horst von Irmer, Munich : 62 l, 63 al, ar & c, 110 a, 111, 114 l & br, 116–117, 118 al, 119 ar, 136–137, 150 ar, 235 a, 242 ar, cr & cl, 244–245, 246 a, 247 (2), 250 bc, 251.
laenderpress, Düsseldorf : 22 al, 27 a (Streichan), 194–195.
Franz-Karl Frh. von Linden, Munich : 90–91, 92–93 (4), 94–95 (2).
Magnum, Paris : 66 a, 67 bc.
Mauritius-Verlag, Mittenwald : 44–45 (Bohnacker).
Panam, New York : 197 a.
Paul Popper Foto, London : 131 cl, 143, 230–231 a.
Roger-Viollet, Paris : 122 a, 135 a, 138 l & r, 139 ar, 152–153, 154–155, 156 b, 157 b.
roebild, Frankfurt a.M. : 26.
Salmer, Barcelona : 36–37, 39 ar.
Toni Schneiders, Lindau : 32–33, 38, 39 al.
Karlheinz Schuster, Frankfurt a.M. : 59 ac, 87 a, 96l, 98–99 (IDF-Studio).
Arthur von Schwertführer, Wiesbaden : 230 al, 231 ar.
Shostal, New York : 8–9, 35 b, 48–49, 51 a & b, 60–61, 71 r, 104–105, 120–121, 128–129, 132–133, 140–141, 144–145, 162, 166 b, 172, 178–179, 182–183, 184–185, 192–193, 198–199 (2), 200–201, 204–205, 206 l, 208–209, 211 a, 218–219, 222–223, 225, 228–229, 236–237, 240–241, 248–249.
United Press International, Frankfurt a.M. : 197 br, 218 bl, 232–233, 234 c.
USIS, Bad Godesberg : 224 a. Verkehrsamt Cologne : 20–21 (Hermann Claasen) : 22 ar, 23 (Claus Schmid).
Carl Zeiss, Oberkochen (by arrangement with NASA) : 220 al & bl, 220–221 a.
ZFA, Düsseldorf : 10 a, 24, 106, 123, 131 a, 147, 167 a, 174–175, 177, 215 a & bl, 238 bl, 239.

Black and white
Erich Andres, Hamburg : 230 bl.
Anthony-Verlag, Starnberg : 86 b (Rösch).
Archiv für Kunst und Geschichte, Berlin : 12 al, 14 r, 15 a, 17 ar & cbl.
Associated Press Picture Service, Frankfurt a.M. : 59 b.
Bavaria-Verlag, Gauting : 82 a ; Gerhart Brinkmann : 173 cl ; Comet : 246 & br ; A Ehrhardt : 176 b ; Martin Frank : 226 l, 227 r ; Helmut Heimpel : 173 al & bl ; Konrad Helbig : 50 a & c ; Lebeck : 46 al ; Omnia : 163 br ; Willem van de Poll : 122 ca ; Günther R. Reitz : 122 b, 167 bl & br ; Alfre Rosteck : 196 b ; Silvester : 86a, 110 ac ; Hed Wiesner : 206 ar ; Zahn : 34
Presse-Informations-Agentur Brinzer, Winnenden : 27 b.
dpa-Bild, Frankfurt a.M. : 66 b, 67 b, 218 al & cl.
Expo 67 Montreal, Press Office : 190 (3).
French Tourist Office, Frankfurt a.M. : 82 b (Baranger).
Us Foreign Tourist Agency, Frankfurt a.M. 196 a, 203.
Roland Gööck, Munich (Archiv) : 10 br, 22 bl & br, 34 b, 46 ac, 50 b, 54 br, 107 br, 121 al, 166 a, 197 bl, 206 br, 238 br.
Historia-Foto, Bad Sachsa : 12 b, 14 bl, 17 al, 235 al.
Horst von Irmer, Munich : 250 ac & b.
laenderpress, Düsseldorf : 230–231 a.
Franz-Karkl Frh. von Linden, Munich : 93 r.
Bildarchiv Foto-Marburg, Marburg : 100 b.
Mauritius-Verlag, Mittenwald : 142 ar, 250 a.
Dutch Embassy, Bonn : 30, 31 b (Mastboom Vliegbedrijf, Hofmeester), 31 a (KLM-Aerocarto).
Panama Canal Company, Balboa Heights : 235 br.
S. Pandis (Farabola), Munich : 54 bl.
Paul Popper Foto, London : 42 c, 46 bc, 120 ar, 139 bl, 146 (3), 163 bl, 176 a, 202 (2), 242 al & bl.
Willy Pragher, Freiburg : 87 br.
roebild, Frankfurt a.M. : 88 l (Schneider).
Roger-Viollet, Paris : 10 br, 11 a & c, 15 br, 16 b, 17 cal, 39 bl & br, 42 b, 46 r, 58 b, 59 a, 62–63 c, 101 a, ca & cb, 107 al & cl, 110 b, 114 a 118 bl & br, 119 bl & br, 120 al, 121 ar, 126 (4), 131 bl & br, 135 bl & b 139 al, cal & cbl, 150 l, 152 (3), 156–157 (4), 163 ar & cr, 166 c, 187 a 224 bc & br.
South Africa Tourist Office, Frankfurt a.M. : 178 l, 179 r.
Toni Schneiders, Lindau : 142 al & bl.
Spanish Tourist Office, Frankfurt a.M. : 34 a.
Canadian Tourist Office, Frankfurt a.M. ; 183, 187 ac.
Staatsbibliothek Berlin (Handke) : 12 ar, 14 al, 17 car & cbr.
Suddeutscher Verlag, Picture Service, Munich : 67 a.
Ullstein-Picture-Service, Berlin : 63 b, 67 ca, 70 l, 71 al & cl, 78 bl, 82 c (Camera-Press), 142 br (Gäbele), 150 br, 187 cb & b, 210 l, 231 br, 235 bc.
USIS, Bad Godesberg : 210 ar & br, 211 b, 224 bl.
Verkehrsamt Cologne : 22 c (Theo Felten).
Dr Paul Wolff & Tritschler, Frankfurt a.M. : 214 a.
Yellowstone National Park, Wyoming/USA : 214 b.

Abbreviations : l = left, r = right, a = above, c = centre, b = below.

INDEX

ncerrajes Room 39
 Simbel 166, 166
opolis 60–3, 61, 63
lsburg Grottos 96
a Capitolina 117
ca 159
a 124, 126
uille du Midi' 67
na 37
zaba 38
)schami al Umawi 114
ander the Great 13, 109
andria 17, 17
andria, Pharos of 17, 17
mbra 37–8, 37, 39
ne massif 67
r of Democracy' 202
ing 94
rado Palace 242
hitheatreum Flavium (Colosseum) 50, 50
sterdam 31
alusia 37
kor 137–8
kor Thom 137–8, 137, 138
kor Wat 137–8, 138
esala de Embajadores' 34
pater of Sidon 7
oninus, Temple of 50, 50
llo Programme 218, 221
ilegia 42
de Triomphe 74–5, 75
ic Circle 91
angelski Cathedral 101
dt, Ernst Moritz 42
mis 14
mis at Ephesus, Temple of 14, 14
 103
van High Dam 168, 168
ualpa 248
gatis 109
ena 60
ens 60–3
s Rockets 221
nium 26, 26
ustus 109
ngzeb 124, 126
soluk 14

 108
bek 108–10, 109, 110
el, Tower of 13, 194
ylon 13
ylon, Hanging Gardens of 12–3, 13
chus cult 110
chus, Temple of 109, 110, 110
ecker, Karl 56, 127

Bahret Lut (Lot Lake) 122
Bandeirantes 247
Bangkok 131, 131
Baphuon 137
barays 137
Bartholdi, Frédéric-Auguste 196
Basil's Cathedral, St 101, 101
Bay Bridge (Oakland Suspension Bridge) 224, 225
Bay of Rio 238–9, 239
Bayon 138, 138
Bedloe's Island (Liberty Island) 196
Bekaa Valley 108
Belfort 86
Ben-gavriêl, M. Y. 122
Bernini 55
Bethlehem 119
Big Hole 178–9, 179
Bingham, Hiram 249
Bitter Lake 162
Black Hills 202
Blagoveshchenski Cathedral 102
Blue Mosque 107
Boabdil 37
Bodrum (Halicarnassus) 15, 15
Bohrdt, Hans 187
Boiserée, S. 22
Bönickhausen, Hans Heinrich 69
Borglum, Gutzon 202
Borobudur, Temple of 155–7, 155, 157
Bosphorus 107
Bramante 53
Brand, Adam 153
Brasilia 242–3, 243
Breughel (Tower of Babel) 13
Brooklyn Bridge 225
Brussels 26, 26, 27
Buddha of Kamakura 145–6, 146
Buddhas, Temple of the un-numbered 155
Burckhardt, Jacob 14, 45, 55
Burma 132
Butsu 145

Cajamarca 248
California 209
California, Gulf of 206
Callicrates 62
Calvary, Mount 118
Cambodia 137
Campo vaccino 50
Canada 181
Caracol 231
Caria 15
Cárdenas, Lopez de 206
Cartier, Jacques 183
Castillo, El 230, 231

'Cathedral of Buddhism' 132
Cecrops 63
Chalgrin 75
Chamonix 67
Champs-Elysées 75
Chares 16
Charles V, Emperor 34, 233
Cheops, pyramid of 11, 11
Chephren, pyramid of 11, 11
Chicago 226, 227
Chichen Itza 228–32, 228, 231
China, Great Wall of 150–3, 151
Christ's Nativity, Church of 119
Chrysler Building 195
Chrysostomos 17
Churchill, Lord Randolph 179
Chu Yüan-chang 151
Cimon 61
Circus of Nero 52
Cleopatra 109
Cleveland, President Grover 196
Colesberg Kopje 178
Cologne Cathedral 21–2, 22
Colon 233
Colorado River 206, 207
Colosseum 50, 50
Colossus of Rhodes 16, 16
Comares Tower 38, 39
Constantine the Great, Emperor 52, 106
Constantinople 106
Cook, Thomas 5
Copacabana 239, 239
Corcovado 239, 239
Corning Glassworks 209
Costa, Lucio 242
Courmayer 67
Couturier, M. A. 86
Cristobal 233
Curitiba

dagobas 155, 156
Dai Butsu of Kamakura 145–6, 146
Dai Butsu of Nara 145
Dalton, Herman 214
Damascus 114–5
Dandolo, Enrico 42
Dead Sea 122, 122
Delhi 124
Delta Plan 31
Demetrius Poliorcetes 16
Deussen, Paul 126
Devil's Throat (Garganta do Diablo) 244, 247
Diamond Rush, The Great 178
Dickens, Charles 42
Dinocrates 14
Doge's Palace 42, 42

Dolgoruki, Juri 101
Dome of the Rock *117*, 120, *121*
Dominus flavit chapel *117*
Dos Passos, John 243
Duiveland 31
Dumas, Alexandre 37

Echo River *198*
Edo 142
Eiffel, Alexandre Gustav 68–70, *70*
Eiffel Tower 68–70, 195, 196
Eisenhower Lock *183*
Elephants, Terrace of *138*
Ellis Island 196
Emerald Buddha, Temple of the 131
Empire State Building 195, 196, *195*, *196*
Ephesus, Temple of 14
Erechtheum 62, 63, *63*
Erie, Lake 183, 185
Escorial 34, *34*
Essene 122
Estilo Herreresco 34
Everyman Gorge 94, *94*

Faustina, Temple of 50, *50*
Ferdinand, King 37
Field of Mars 70
Fioraventi 101
Fiorelli, Giuseppe 59
Firehole River 214
Fischer von Erlach 7
'five fingers' 172
Florida 218
Flowers, Mountain of 133
Foucher 155
Friedell, Egon 166
Friedländer, Ludwig 50

Gagarin, Yuri 219
Gaillard Cut 234, *234*
Gatun, Lake *233*, 234
Geitskór, Grim 94
Gemini Programme 219
Genghis Khan 151
Gero cross 22
Gethsemane, Garden of *119*, 119
Gibrat, Robert 82
Giorgione 42
Gizeh, Pyramids of 11, *11*
Glockner-Kaprun 24, *24*
Goat Island 185
Goethals, George Washington 233
Goethe, Johan Wolfgang von 19, 22, 42, 79
Golden Gate, Jerusalem 119
Golden Gate Bridge 224–5, *225*
Golden Mountain 133
Golgotha 117
Granada 117
Grand Canal 42, *42*
Grand Canyon 206–7, *207*
Great Diamond Rush 178
'Great Terrace' *214*
Great Lakes 183, 185

Great Wall of China 150–3, *151*, *153*
Green River 206
Grevelingen dam *31*
Grissom, Astronaut 219
Grossglockner 24, *24*
Guaira Falls 244
Guarnari 244

Haas, Wily 16, 19
Habitat 190–1, *191*
Hadad 109
Hadschar el Hubla 108, *110*
Hagia Sofia 106–7, *107*
Hale, George Ellery 209
Hale Telescope *210*
Halicarnassus 15, *15*
Hamet 38
Hanging Gardens of Babylon 12–3, *13*
Haram al Sharif 119
Hardouin-Mansart, Jules 78
Haringuliet Dam 31
Hauff, von 247
Heims, P. G. 145
Helena, Empress 117
Heliopolis 109
Helios 16
Hennepin, Louis 185
Herculaneum 59, *59*
Herodotus 11
Herostratus 14
Herrera, Juan de 34
Hesse-Wartegg, Ernst von 5, 47, 101, 152
Hielscher, Kurt 39
Hildebold, Archbishop 21
Holy Fig Tree, Temple of the 131
Holy Sepulchre 117
Holy Sepulchre, Church of the 118–19, *121*
Home Insurance Building 194
Hooker Telescope 209
Hopeh 150
Huang Ho (Yellow River) 150
Huascar 248
Huayna Capac 248
Hulagu 110
Huron, Lake 183

Iceland 91–93, *91*
Ictinus 62
Iemitsu 142
Ieyasu 142
Iguaçu Falls 244, *244*, 247, *247*
Iguaçu River 244, *244*
Incas 248, *249*
Indian Republic 244
Isabella, Queen 37
Isidoros of Miletus 106
Ismail Pasha 162
Istanbul 107, *107*
Ivan the Terrible 101

Java 155
Jayavarman VII 137–8
Jeannerat, Charles Edouard (Le Corbusier) 86

Jefferson, Thomas 202, *202*
Jenny, Major Le-Baron 194
Jerusalem 117–21, *117*, *119*, *121*
Johann, A. E. 157, 172, 238
John, Order of St 15
John the Baptist 144
Jordan River 122
Joseph of Arimathea 119
Josephus, Flavius 12
Julius II, Pope 53
Jupiter, Temple of 109, 110
Jupiter Heliopolitanus 110
Justinian, Emperor 106

Kalat al-Hambra 37
Kalita, Grand Duke Ivan Danilovitch 101
Kamakura, Dai Butsu of 145–6, *146*
Kansu 150
Kaprun Valley 24, *24*
Kariba Dam 176, *176*
Kariba Valley 176
Karst 96
Kemal Ataturk 107
Kennedy, Cape 218–21, *219*
Kentucky 198
Khalid Ibn Walid 114
Khmer 137, *137*
Khuan, Ernst von 110
Kimberley 178
Kircher, Athanasius 7
Klenze, Leo von 62
Kochba, Ben 117
Koldeway, Robert 13
Königsmarck, Count 62
Konrad of Hochstaden, Archbishop 21
Kremlin 101, *101*
Kubitschek de Oliveira, President Juscelina 242,
243
Kulkulkan, Temple of (El Castillo) 230, *231*
Kutschka, Stepan 101
Kutschovo 101

Lady of Paris' 68
Laki 91
La Rance Tidal Power Station 82, *82*
La Salle 185
Laussier *187*
Lebanon 108
Le Brun 78
Le Corbusier 86
Lenin Mausoleum 101, *101*
Le Nôtre 78
Leo III, Pope 52
Lesseps, Vicomte Ferdinand de 162, *162*, 233
Le Vau 78
Liberty, Statue of 196, *196*
Lido 42
Lincoln, Abraham 202, *202*
Lincoln Building 196
Lion Courtyard *37*, 39
Lion Fountain *39*
Litschaver, Franz 34
Livingstone, Dr David 172
Lochner, Stephen 22

Lake 122
s XIII 78
s XIV 78, 79
s XVI 79
s Philippe 74
wig I of Bavaria 62
ow, Carl von 55

s River 31
chine of Marley' 78
hu Picchu 248–50, 249, 250
erna, Carlo 55
inet Isa 115
onnina 46, 47
rid 34
d of the Mist 187
aux, André 243
mmoth Caves 198, 198
co Capac 248
hattan Island 194
n, Thomas 42
nekin Pis 26
co Polo 131, 151
garitze Reservoir 24, 24
na City 226–7, 227
nagen 69
seillaise' (Rudé) 75
en de Vos 7
ré 22
passant, Guy de 70
azin 120
a 288
aliths 88
gale ekklesia 106
r-Graefe, Julius 166
ille 56
an River 131
cury Programme 219
t Island 221
elangelo 53
n Cathedral 45–7, 47
amoto no Yoritomo 145
lon Min, King 132
Avenue 153
Dynasty 150–3
guzzi, Luciano 46
flores 233, 234
ones 244
sicles 62
ammed (Prophet) 120
ammed I 37
ammed V 37
t Blanc Tunnel 67, 67
t Cenis Tunnel 67
te de la Asabica 37
te Somma 57, 57
treal 190–1
t St Michel 82
cow 101, 101
erboden 24, 24
hout, Henri 137
nt of Olives 120, 121
taz-i-Mahal 124
solini, Benito 46
erinos, Pyramid of 11

Myrtle Courtyard 38, 39

Naples 56, 57
Napoleon I 45, 74, 162
Nara, Dai Butsu of 145
NASA 218
Nasser, Lake 166, 168
Nats 133
Navaho Indian 207
Nebuchadnezzar 12–3
Nefertari 166, 166
Negrelli, Alois 162
Nero 50
New York 194–6, 195, 196
Niagara Falls 185–7, 185, 187
Niagara River 185
Nicholas V, Pope 53
Niemeyer, Oscar 242
Nike, Temple of 62, 63
Nikko 142, 143, 143
Nile River 166, 168
Niomen Gate 143
Nirvana 156
Novacap 242
Novi, Alevisio 101
'nunnery' (Chichen Itza) 231
Nyeglinnaia 101

Oakland Suspension Bridge 224, 225
Old Faithful 214, 215
Olives, Mount of 121
Olympia 17
Omar, Caliph 117
Omar, Mosque of 120
Omayyad Mosque 114–5, 115
Ono Goroemon 145
Ontario, Lake 183, 185
Oosterschelde Bridge 31, 31
Orion nebula 210
Overflakkee 31
Öxará Waterfall 94

Pages, George 79
Palacio arabe (Alhambra) 38
Palacio del Generalife 38
Palomar, Mount 209–10
Palomar Observatory, Mount 209–10, 209, 210
Panama, Isthmus of 233
Panama Canal 233–4, 233, 234
Papal Altar 55
Paraguay 244
Paraná 244
Paraná River 244
Paris 68
Parterre de Latonne 79
Parthenon 61, 62, 63
Pasadena 210
Pasterze glacier 24
Pa-ta-ling 151
Paul III, Pope 55
Paul V, Pope 55
Peacock Throne 124
'pearl of Andalusia' 37

Pedro Miguel 234
Pericles 61
'Persian rubble' 61
Peter (Apostle) 52
Peter, Citadel of 15
Peter, Metropolitan 101
Petrarch 42
Pharos of Alexandria 17, 17
Phidias 17, 61
Philip II 34
Philocles 63
Pinacotheca 62
Pizarro, Francisco 248
Place de l'Etoile 75
Planalto Palace 243, 243
Pliny 14
Poghliaghi, Lodovico 46
Polo, Marco 131, 151
Pompeii 59, 59
Ponte Sant'Angelo 55
Popa, Mount 133
Porto Iguazú 244
Poseidon 60
Poseidon Erechtheus 62
Postojna Cave 96, 96
Potter, Stephen 194
Powell, Major J. W. 206
Priestley, J. B. 207
'Prince's grave' 250
Puerta de los Sieta Suelos 37
Pyramids of Gizeh 11, 11

Quadras 242
Qumran 122

Rainald of Dassel, Archbishop 21
Rama I 131
Rameses II 166, 166
Rance River 82
Rangoon 132
Raphael 55
Rawstorne, Fleetwood 178
RCA Building 196
Reclining Buddha 131, 131
Red Sea 162, 162
Red Square 101, 101
'reductions' 244
Remus 50, 52
Rennequin, René 78
Republica de Panama 233
Reykjavik 94
Rhine River 31
Rhodes 16
Rhodesia 176
Rialto Bridge 42
Rieker, Heinrich 221
Rieppel, Paul 11
Rio de Janeiro 238–9, 239
Rio de la Plata 244
Rockefeller Centre 196, 196
'Rock of Lot's Wife' 122
Rocky Mountains 214
Roman Forum 50, 50
Rome, Ancient 50, 50, 53, 55

Romulus 50, 52
Ronchamp 86, *86*
Rosse's telescope, Lord 210
Roosevelt, Theodore 202, *202*, 234
Rossellino, Bernardo 53
Rudé (Marseillaise) *75*
Rushmore. Mount 202, *202*

Sadd el Aali 168
Safdie, Moshe 190
Said Pasha 162
St Gotthard Tunnel 67
St Lawrence 34
St Lawrence River 183
St Lawrence Seaway 183, *183*
St Malo 82
St Mark's Church 42, *42*
St Mark's Square 42, *42*
St Peter's Church 52–5, *53*, *55*
St Peter's Square *53*, 55, *55*
St Servan 82
Saint-Suliac 82, *82*
Saladin, Sultan 110, 117
'Salt Sea' 122
Saluzza, Antonio de 46
San Francisco 224–5, *225*
Sangallo, Giuliano de 55
San Pietro, Piazza di 55
San Pietro in Vaticano 52
São Sebastiao do Rio de Janeiro 238
Saturn I rocket 219
Saturn V rocket 221
Schelde River 31
Schipol 31
Seine River *79*
Seleucids 109
Seljuks 117
Semiramis 12–3, *13*
Semiramis, Hanging Gardens of 12
Sepp, Father 244
Serro da Mar 244
Shah Jahan 124, 126
Shan-hai-kuan 150
Shepard, Alan 219
Shi Huang Ti, Emperor 150
Shwe Dagon Pagoda 132–4, *133*, *134*
Sierra de Guadarrama 34
Simplon Tunnel 67
Singer Building 194
Sostratus 17
South Dakota 202
Sphinx *11*
Sputnik 1 218
Stabiae 59
Statue of Liberty 196, *196*
Stonehenge 88, *88*

'Stone of the Pregnant Woman' 108, *110*
Strabo 57
stupa 155
Sturyavarman II 137
Su-chou 150
Suez Canal 162, *162*
Sugar Loaf Mountain 238
'Sun King' 78
'Sun Observatory' *250*
Superior, Lake 183
Surtsey 91–3, *93*
Surtur 91, *91*, *93*
Suspiro del Moro, El 37
Sylvester I, Pope 52

Taj Mahal 124–7, *127*
Tamerlane 110, 115
Tiber River *55*
Timsah, Lake *162*
Tintoretto 42
Titan II rocket *219*
Titian 42
Titus 117
Titus' Arch *50*
Thailand 131, 137
Thatcher Ferry Bridge *234*
Themistocles 61
Theodosius, Emperor 110, 114
Thingvellir 94, *94*
Thompson, D'Arcy Wentworth 190
Three Island Plan 31
Three Kings, Shrine of the 22, *22*
'Three Windows, Temple of the' *250*
Todaiji 145
Tokugawa 142
Tokyo 142, 145–6
Toledo, Juan Bautista de 34
Toltecs 230
Toshogu 142, *143*
Toynbee, Arnold 228
Trevithick 68
Tutankhamun *166*

UN Building *195*, 196
Urban II, Pope 46
Urubamba 249
Uspenski Cathedral 101
Uxmal 228

Varro 50
Venice 42, *42*
Venus, Temple of *109*
Verne, Jules 82
Verona, Gioconda da 55

Veronese 42
Verrazano Narrows Bridge 224
Versailles 78–9, *79*
Vesuvius 56–9, *57*, *59*
Via Dolorosa 119, *119*
Victoria Falls 172–3, *176*
Vigano, Vico 45–6
Virgin River 206
Visconti, Giovanni Galeazzo 45

Wailing Wall 118, *121*
Walid, Khalim ibd 114
Warriors, Temple of the *228*, 230, *231*
Washington, George 202
Wasserfall 24
Wat Arun *131*
Wat Benchamabopitr *131*
Wat Phra Kaeo 131, *131*
Wat Po 131, *131*
Webb, James E. 218
Wellington, Duke of 38
White, astronaut *221*
Wilhelm II, Emperor 110
Wilson Observatory, Mount 209
Wiltshire 88
Wood, J. T. 14
World Exhibition (1899) 68
World Fair (1958) 27
World Fair (1967) 190

Xerez, Francisco de 248

Yellow Sea 150
Yellow River (Huang Ho) 150
Yellowstone Lake 214
Yellowstone National Park 214
Yellowstone River 214, *214*
Yomeimon Gate *143*
Young, astronaut 219
Yucatan 228

Zambezi River 172–3, *173*, 176, *176*
Zambia 176
Zangi, Emir 110
Zar Kolokol *101*
Zebedani 108
Zeus, Statue of 17, *17*
Zimbabwe 159
Zuider Zee 31